Finishing Well

Retirement Skills
for Ministers

Fourth Edition

The Living Well Series, Volume 1

The Living Well Series

(See http://www.pastorselfcare.com)

Volume 1: *Finishing Well: Retirement Skills for Ministers.*
Available at www.createspace.com/3789682. Ministers face much more difficult retirement issues than most secular individuals. They not only lose their occupation, but they often lose friends, identity, self-esteem and too frequently, even their future hope of effective ministry. This book provides ministers with skills to know when it is time to retire, how to gracefully transition to a new ministry, and how to survive and thrive like never before.

Volume 2: *Transforming Conflict: Relationship Skills for Ministers.*
Available at www.createspace.com/3856947. This book helps ministers prevent church discord even while enhancing relationships. This book helps individuals learn:
- How to prevent and eliminate relationship obstacles
- How to cultivate research-proven relationship skills
- How to adapt each relationship skill to their ministry

Volume 3: *Rebound From Burnout: Resilience Skills for Ministers.*
Available at www.createspace.com/3854604. This book equips ministers with resilience skills (physical, emotional, and spiritual resilience) to prevent and recover from burnout.

Volume 4: *Transforming Personality: Spiritual Formation and the Five-Factor Model.* Available at www.createspace.com/3925645.
By integrating the spiritual disciplines with assessment tools, this book shows how to use the Five-Factor Personality Model to assess personality, fruit of the Spirit, motivational gifts of the Spirit, ministry aptitudes, vocational aptitudes, and styles of behavior.

Volume 5: *Transforming Shattered Dreams: Hope for Wounded Parents in Global Service.* Available at www.createspace.com/4216990.
This book provides hope for parents of prodigal children.

Volume 6: *Rebound From Crisis: Resilience for Crisis Survivors.*
Available at www.createspace.com/3935466. This book provides the same resilience skills as Volume 3. However, Volume 6 is designed specifically for church members.

Volume 7: *The New Birth Transition: Conquering Rejection.*
Available at www.createspace.com/4391591. This book provides new Christians with skills to profess their faith in cultures that tend to disdain Christians.

Volume 8: *Abusive Power: When Christians Hurt Other Christians.*
Available at www.createspace.com/4796808. This book helps Christians recover from abusive power-based behaviors.

Finishing Well

Retirement Skills
for Ministers

Fourth Edition

The Living Well Books, Volume 1

By Nathan Davis
and
Beth Davis, D.Min.

Cover photo and all other photos by iStockphoto

Fourth Edition

ISBN-13: 978-1470024222
ISNS-10: 1470024225

Printed in USA

To Mom and Dad

Acknowledgments

 The retirement of my missionary parents, Dr. Jim and Genevieve Davis, inspired me to write this book. After forty-eight years of missionary service in Asia and Europe, they suddenly retired. During the first few weeks after their decision, I remember my father reflecting that he felt emotionally overwhelmed by his loss of identity. My parent's candid insights into their deepest emotions revealed that a minister's retirement remains fundamentally different than that of secular individuals.

I am convinced that God delayed my parent's retirement until their mid-seventies so they could provide the unique insights needed for this book. They retired extremely well but the process initially bewildered us all. Dr. Jim and Genevieve Davis continue to serve as an ideal inspiration of how to retire successfully. They are still foreign missionaries. They never lost their true identity—they simply added a new *secular* label called *retired* and decided to forgo monetary payment for their labor. Because Mom and Dad never lost their *call,* they continue working as ministers until the day that God offers them a true retirement. I thank them for including me in their retirement planning process and helping me understand what lays ahead for all ministers.

Nathan Davis

Table of Contents

CHAPTER 1

What Is Successful Retirement Transition?

I never stopped doing anything [when I retired], I stopped getting paid for it. — Bill Chavannel

Three Fundamental Retirement Questions

When 89-year-old Rev. Duel Tanner was asked, "For you, what was the scariest aspect of retirement?" he quickly responded, "Facing it. I really didn't know what to expect."

Many ministers (especially missionaries and chaplains) scarcely know what to expect as they face retirement. Transition *can* mean excitement, adventure, a sense of fresh leading from the Lord, and a brand new, long-anticipated opportunity. Like your initial training in ministry, however, you will greatly benefit from thorough planning and hard work. We hope this book will help you through that planning process.

As you progress through this book, we hope to help you answer three fundamental retirement questions:

1. What does it mean for a minister to retire successfully?
2. What can each minister do to successfully accomplish this important life task?
3. In what ways can your agency make changes to enable ministers to retire more successfully?

Since the transition process varies greatly among individuals, you may not need to address in great detail some issues discussed in this book. However, do not ignore the other parts. The process of working through the material that seems less important often prevents more serious issues from developing at a later stage of transition.

What is Successful Retirement for a Minister?

As described in this book, successful retirement for a minister occurs when the individual is able to thrive physically, vocationally, socially, and spiritually in retirement. Successful retirement for a minister requires reframing four (potentially new) ways to think about his or her identity as a retired minister.

First, successful retirement requires breaking out of the "disease treatment" approach common in North America and a few other cultures. Only two percent of North Americans consider the age over sixty as the best in life, while thirty percent of those between age eighteen and sixty-four consider retirement age as the least desirable (Harris et. al., 1975). Although thirty percent of North Americans describe retirement as the least desirable stage of life, successful retirement is NOT a treatment plan for individuals who, because of age, have finally grown inactive, disabled, or marginalized. That is, retired ministers are NOT infected with some disease called outdated or old age!

Contrary to common belief, successful retirement has nothing to do with the medical or emotional treatment of individuals who have finally passed an age threshold. That mentality simply enables psychological abuse of one of God's most promising resources.

In Japan, where I was raised as a missionary kid (MK), the culture highly values and honors the elderly for their wisdom. The strong cultural value of seeking advice from the elderly provides them with a highly valued role in society. Corporations seek the elderly for leadership positions, and newly married couples regularly seek advice from the eldest in the family. In Japan, the elderly truly live an esteemed role.

In comparison to many world cultures, the North American culture often systematically destroys the self-image of retirement age ministers with an "illness treatment" mentality. In North America, the elderly (and especially ministers) are commonly pushed into retirement sooner than others, as if they contracted some terrible disease. Retirement age ministers tell me that even other ministers sometimes treat them as "has-beens." Many local churches question the ability of retirement age ministers, and endorse the young ministers as the most desirable. The outlook for retired missionaries and chaplains looks even worse. Thus, we hope to resist treating any retirement aged minister as marginalized.

Second, successful retirement for a minister requires focusing on identity issues. When secular individuals prepare for retirement, they often focus on financial planning to live comfortably on a reduced income. For them, retirement planning centers on financial planning. For ministers, however, finances rarely represent the most important retirement issue. After all, very few ministers enter the ministry because they value and want to pursue financial wealth or an easy lifestyle.

Most people enter ministry because they feel "called by God" for a lifetime of service. The call to minister represents a deep part of the minister's core identity. Ministry is not simply something that we do, it represents who we are, at the core. As a person called by God, I experience spiritual growth that develops my love, joy, peace, patience, kindness, goodness, faithfulness, gentleness and self-control (the fruit of the Spirit). Over a lifetime of service and walking with God, I gradually mature into a different person. My core identity changes.

Since most ministers feel called for a lifetime of service, the call rarely ends at retirement. Retirement may cause a reduction in income, but it never changes the minister's motives or internal values. When asked about his or her occupation, a retired secular person will usually say, "I am retired." More rarely he or she will say, "I am a retired …(carpenter, postman, engineer, teacher, etc.). When queried about his or her occupation, however, a retired minister will usually say, "I am a minister." We see ourselves as a minister for life, not just until retirement.

At retirement, many ministers not only risk losing their occupation, but if they need to leave their local congregation, they risk losing friends, self-esteem and too frequently, even their future hope of effective ministry. So a loss of identity represents the most significant risk for a minister. And the minister's identity is worth more than any amount of money. For most ministers, their identity is worth more than life, itself. For a minister, successful retirement means focusing on identity issues even more than money issues. The loss of identity can lead to intense guilt, self-blame, ruminating on past regrets, depression, and physical illness. Thus, a minister risks a much deeper loss than risked by most secular individuals. This book focuses on identity issues.

When facing retirement, secular individuals fear a loss of income— Ministers fear a loss of identity.

Third, successful retirement for a minister requires developing plans to thrive like never before. Fifty years ago, the average sixty-five year old retiree retained less than five years of life expectancy. Due to his short life expectancy, the culture of that day considered a sixty-five year old retiree as old. Currently, the average sixty-five year old still retains about one-quarter of his or her life expectancy. Therefore, age sixty-five to eighty is no longer considered "old"—it simply offers new opportunities. No one gets old until he or she passes eighty years of age, at the least.

Many do not consider themselves old until age ninety or later. This book probably will not help ministers who consider themselves old. It is intended to help those who consider themselves seniors—those nearing retirement who still remember their call into life-long ministry and service.

"Old Age" is a psychological notion—
it is not a numerical age.

In contrast to the common image of retirees in North America, successful retirement embodies the intentional planning and development of a new lifestyle in which the retired minister grows more productive and thrives more than any prior chapter of life. Many successful retirees reach their most productive years after they reach retirement age. For instance:

- John Glenn, America's first astronaut, was seventy-seven years old when he made his last journey in space. Prior to that, he became a U.S. senator, but only after he had retired from NASA.

- Doris Haddock was ninety-one years old when she walked 3200 miles across the United States.

- Grandma Moses began to paint in her late seventies.

- George Bernard Shaw continued to write until his death at age ninety-four. One of his most popular works is "My Fair Lady."

- Agatha Christie wrote mystery novels for over fifty years.

- Golda Meir was sworn in as the prime minister of Israel at the age of sixty-three.

- Michelangelo, at age seventy-one, completed his greatest work—St. Peter's Basilica.

- Benjamin Franklin was the oldest delegate to sign the Declaration of Independence. He lived to be eighty-four years old.

- Andy Rooney and Mike Wallace both served as prime-time television personalities beyond their eighty-eighth birthdays.

- Dr. C. Everett Koop served as one of America's most outstanding surgeon generals from age sixty-five to age seventy-three.

- Ellen Glasgow, who won the Pulitzer Prize at age sixty-seven, said, "In the past few years, I have made a thrilling discovery…that until one is over sixty, one can never really learn the secret of living."

- Mother Teresa received the Nobel Peace Prize at the age of sixty-nine. Afterward, she continued working and establishing new missions until she died at age eighty-seven.

- John Bertram Phillips, a well-known Bible translator, published *The Wounded Healer* at age seventy-eight.

- At the ages of 104 and 102, sisters Sarah and Dr. Bessie Delany wrote the New York Times bestseller, *Having Our Say: The Delany Sisters' First 100 Years*. At the ages of 105 and 103, they published a sequel. At age 107, Sarah Delany published another sequel, *On My Own at 107*.

Fourth, successful retirement for a minister requires exercising creativity that already exists. Gene Cohen, Director of the Center on Aging, Health and Humanities at George Washington University, reports: "Creative output is influenced more by experience in a field—'career age'—than by chronological age" (Cohen, 2000, 108). If Cohn is correct, the retirement age minister is at his or her creative zenith. No wonder that seniors in the above list accomplished their greatest feats after age sixty.

The minister who successfully transitions into retirement can offer more to the Kingdom of God after retirement than at any previous time of life.

To help you reframe the above four ways of thinking about your identity as a retirement eligible minister, we invite you to develop four critically important support legs (edited from Rowe and Kahn, *Successful Aging*, 1999, 39) that sustain a successful retirement:

1. Physical health
2. A growing intimacy with God
3. Social interaction
4. Meaningful ministry

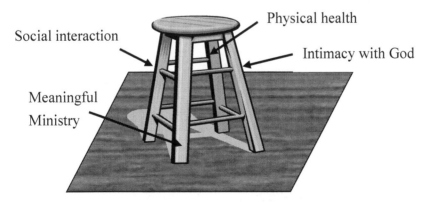

Figure 1: The four support legs of successful retirement

What is Successful Transition?

Transition is a phase at which events and environment alter our roles, relationships, routines, and assumptions. Although ministerial life involves many transitions, *retirement transition* significantly alters the roles, relationships, routines, and assumptions for almost every minister, especially for missionaries and chaplains. The minister's identity may remain unchanged, but his or her roles, relationships, routines, and assumptions may change greatly.

Unfortunately, many ministers spend mental and emotional energy worrying about the *change* that thrusts them into retirement. That change may include loss of physical health, loss of job, loss of status, loss of social prominence, or any number of other causative factors. The change results from an external factor, event, or environment mostly outside of their control. Although a change may stimulate your transition into retirement, focusing your energy on factors that remain outside of your control usually remains unproductive.

Retirement transition has the potential to alter your future more positively or more negatively than any other life transition.

Change results from an external factor. However, we refer to transition as an internal factor. Transition reflects an internal adjustment of attitudes and assumptions. You are the only individual who retains control over your attitudes and assumptions. This book invites you to process the normal retirement transition emotions caused by change and to choose new attitudes that refocus your energy and resources on transition. The objective of this book is to empower you with skills to control not your change but your transition.

Debunking "Disengagement Theory"

Rowe and Kahn (*Successful Aging*) provide the following explanation of a commonly accepted distortion of truth:

> Thirty years ago, something called "disengagement theory" was influential among gerontologists. This theory defined the main task of old age as letting go. The argument was that old age was a time at which people were required to give up their jobs, could no longer take part in the more strenuous forms of recreation, and sadly, had to say farewell to many old friends and family members. The final act of relinquishment was letting go of life itself (1999, 46).

In short, disengagement theory portrayed successful retirement transition simply as a time for letting go. Since "letting go" represents only a minor aspect of retirement, it is an untruth (a lie promoted by secular society) whenever it remains unbalanced with the more significant truths about retirement. Indeed, a treatment to help retirees "let go" without the offer of positive replacement behaviors almost guarantees dysfunction and emotional disease among those transitioning into retirement.

Disengagement theory ignores a central retirement truth: you, the prospective retiree, can substantially alter the effects of age through lifestyle choices that increase your well-being, developing an even more meaningful ministry. There is little reason for you to focus on "letting go" during retirement, except to let go of middle-age behaviors and attitudes that hinder you from thriving physically, emotionally and spiritually. There is every reason to focus on replacement attitudes and behaviors that will help you thrive like never before during retirement.

For instance, Rowe and Kahn (1999) eloquently present the following insights: 1) it is often assumed that individuals will gain weight as they age and that weight is affected by heritability. However, two-thirds of weight is governed by lifestyle choices involving diet and exercise. So, there is no reason for you to focus on "letting go" of the expectation to maintain a healthy body weight. In similar fashion, 2) triglyceride levels substantially affect one's susceptibility to heart attacks, but triglyceride levels are determined entirely by lifestyle choices, not genetics. Thus, it appears that lifestyle choices cause heart attacks more than genetics or age. There is no reason for you to "let go" of the expectation that you can maintain a healthy heart after retirement. 3) Lung function substantially predicts one's longevity, but lifestyle choices almost always affect lung function more than genetic influences. 4) Even mental acuity is affected by your lifestyle choices as much as by genetic influences. So, there is little reason for you to "let go" of health expectations during retirement.

As a retiree, you retain lifestyle choices that substantially control all four of the support legs of successful retirement. Successful transition is a process of planning and implementing successful lifestyle choices that promote your wellbeing in the next phase of life. Although this certainly includes "letting go" of some previous lifestyles, it also invites an intentional selection of constructive replacement lifestyles. In short, successful transition invites you to plan for change in nearly every aspect of your life.

Pursuing Physical Health

Transitioning from a full-time ministry to a retirement lifestyle offers an opportunity for you to improve substantially the components of physical health. For instance, old age usually prolongs recovery from ministerial stresses and occupational disabilities that you contracted over the past few decades of ministry. However, in retirement transition, you control an opportunity to plan intentionally how to pursue health and prevent additional disease and disability—this remains a lifestyle choice.

My missionary parents illustrated some lifestyle choices that promote retirement. Although this couple persisted as active missionaries for over a decade longer than most ministers, they eventually found difficulty with traveling. Physicians diagnosed each of them with a different but incurable and progressive life-threatening disease. Discontent with relinquishing their call to missionary service, they armed themselves with volumes of material on slowing the disability that commonly goes along with their respective diseases and armed themselves with knowledge on how to avoid other diseases. They chose a new lifestyle of strict medications, healthy diet, daily exercise, frequent medical checkups, and intentional social interaction, all of which are shown to slow the symptoms of their particular diseases. Long after retirement, they continue to mentor younger Christians. Although this couple will eventually grow physically unable to continue even with this ministry, they made intentional lifestyle choices to pursue health, including as much as possible, preventing additional disease and disability. Even though they contracted incurable diseases, they chose to retire successfully.

Depending on your climate and cultural exposure, you may or may not successfully avoid disease while serving in your previous assignments. However, each minister retains a lifestyle choice to take positive steps to prevent additional disease after retirement. Successful retirement is based largely on that choice—a choice to pursue positive lifestyle changes.

Pursuing Meaningful Ministry

Retirement, job change, and a change in geographical locations may also alter your cognitive function and meaningful ministry. However, as a minister in retirement transition, you retain the opportunity to identify new sources of cognitive stimulation and ministry—it is a lifestyle choice. Missionary "B" provides a great example of this. Following her missionary husband's untimely death, she transferred from a remote area to a missions-based university. When, five years later, she met and married a non-missionary, she had to resign from full-time missionary status because of policies then in place at the agency. Nonetheless, she agreed with the university to continue her work stateside. She has continued this ministry for over thirty years, helping to develop many courses. Over the past three decades, thousands of foreign students have been blessed by her work. Now in her late-seventies, she is still as mentally sharp and productive as at any previous time in her life. When forced to make decisions about her future, she made lifestyle choices that enriched her life with meaningful ministry. And several years ago she embraced yet another challenging missionary ministry, at which time her mission agency restored her full missionary status. While in her retirement years, she continues to produce valuable work at a high cognitive level.

Many ministers (especially missionaries and chaplains) retire earlier than expected due to age-related diseases and other factors that they never anticipated. Factors outside their control prevent them from continuing in their previous ministry. For them, to retire successfully simply means that they retire (transition) to a different ministry than their previous ministry. However, it never means giving up ministry altogether. As individuals called by God, they simply transition to new avenues in which to serve even with their unexpected restrictions. As they become less able to fulfill their ministerial call, they gradually transition to yet another ministry. They retire successfully and thrive cognitively because they adapt to the never-ending process of ministry transition.

Pursuing Social Interaction

Retirement usually dramatically changes a minster's social and support networks, especially those of a missionary or chaplain. However, in retirement transition you can develop opportunities to identify and pursue entirely new patterns of social support—this remains a lifestyle choice. Couple "C" offers a positive example of this. Upon reaching age sixty-five, their agency required them to retire. Discontent with the prospect of isolation from their longtime friends, they purchased a home with a large walk-out basement. After remodeling the basement into fairly luxurious living quarters with a separate entry, full bathroom, living room, and modern kitchen, they offered the new apartment to ministers who need pastoral care and to missionaries on furlough. For the past ten years, they have enjoyed ministering to a constant rotation of close friends returning "home." Recently, they purchased several acres and another home in which they hope to expand their ministry. Instead of languishing in isolation with little social support, they created a strong social support network with what they call their "true" family—other minister friends.

Successful retirement almost always requires lifestyle choices that result in dramatic lifestyle changes. Retention of your past lifestyle rarely results in a successful retirement. Indeed, the success depends on your willingness to adapt to a lifestyle of change. This involves a series of choices to prevent additional disease and disability, engage others socially in a widening support network, and thrive cognitively in meaningful ministry.

Successful retirement transition occurs as you intentionally plan and rebuild each of the above four support legs into a new lifestyle, one that retains and promotes each leg as much or more than at any prior time of your life.

Pursuing Ever Greater Intimacy with God

When Dr. Jim Davis retired after forty-eight years of successful missionary service, he was asked, "What is your greatest regret after reflecting on your previous years of missionary service?" He replied, "That I didn't spend more time with God, getting to know Him more intimately." (Dr. Davis' response seems even more notable to me since I consider him as the most spiritual missionary I know.) Yet, Dr. Davis' regret probably represents the most common response among ministers, worldwide, who transition into retirement. After a lifetime focused on service, they refocus their priorities to their highest priority—a growing intimacy with God.

Due to age, ministers often feel unable to travel and endure physically the rigors of a youthful ministry. However, many retired ministers report a closer relationship with God than ever before. Their ministry grows more dependent on spiritual intimacy than on physical endurance. Without any doubt, their most meaningful ministry occurs as the retiree draws ever closer to God, letting Him lead and inspire every aspect of life. Life-stage transition often impels them to reassess their intimacy with God, as noted by Dr. Beth Davis, missionary director of Healthcare Ministries:

> We met on our first day of class—clinical pastoral education. It was a small group—six of us who would travel together in hospital chaplaincy training for at least one year. As my colleague shared his story with the group, I learned that he had spent twenty-five years as a Presbyterian minister and military chaplain. He loves a good Bible study, and confesses to getting up at 5:00 a.m. each morning with his wife to watch a fiery, female TV evangelist. He is the kind of person who has natural pastoral skills. He exudes warmth and openness; he is approachable—the kind of person most anyone would go to in a crisis to find an understanding heart, a listening ear.

Some time into the middle of our year together, my colleague contracted a terminal form of cancer. From that time on, he became even more transparent with our small group than in the past. In one of our discussions, he exclaimed, "What I wrestle with the most is that I do not love God!" He went on to explain that he loves his wife, his children, his friends— because he sees them, touches them, and interacts with them in tangible ways. However, God is not "there" and does not seem "tangible;" so, how is he to love Him? Wow, I was dumbfounded. How could this godly man, for whom I had so much respect and even love, admit that he did not love God?

Many years later, my colleague's honest and startling statement continues to plague me. Do I love God? Do I know how to love God? Both the Old and New Testaments instruct us to love God. Jesus said that of all the commandments, the most important is, "Love the Lord your God with all your heart and with all your soul and with all your mind and with all your strength" (Mark 12:30). Yet, it is so much easier to approach the second most important commandment, "Love your neighbor as yourself." As my colleague pointed out, "neighbors are tangible."

So, life-stage transition often causes ministers to reflect on their most meaningful relationship. Most ministers well know how to connect with God. We simply get too busy to pursue it consistently. Retirement transition offers a great time to build new habits for spending consistent and prolonged time with God. Dr. Davis continues with another reflection:

Even before walking into the six-year-old patient's room, I had read her medical diagnosis: acute leukemia and Down's Syndrome. As I arrived that morning, her little body twisted and turned as the nurse struggled to adjust her IV. Her mother looked up and quickly came over to greet me. She was a warm, outgoing person, and we easily struck up a conversation. She explained that her daughter had come into the hospital for a blood transfusion; her greatest fear was the IV needles. At that point, her daughter began to scream, and the mother quickly went to her side, attempting to calm her down. Obviously, it was not a good time for a pastoral visit. I quietly left the room. I visited a couple of other patients, and then returned when things had calmed down.

When I returned, this six-year-old patient was an adorable and happy little girl, now waiting to go home. Her mother explained to me that due to so much illness, her daughter was delayed in her ability to speak. Therefore, the whole family studied sign language. From the time when she was just a little over one year old, she was able to understand and speak with signs. Soon, her mother began teaching her about Jesus, and how to pray. At one point, when she was still very young, her mother signed to her, "Jesus lives in heaven." The little girl quickly signed back: "No, Jesus lives here," covering her heart with her little hand.

The patient's mother and I talked a bit about the beauty of children and their understanding of faith. It seems that her daughter did not need anyone to tell her that Jesus lived inside her! Her mother continued to tell me that her daughter loved to pray and seemed to have a great deal of faith. I then began to talk with the little girl about her world, so full of its ups and downs. The conversation flowed naturally as the family prepared to leave the hospital. I wished them well, and then I asked the child, "Would you like to say a prayer with me?" "Sure," she answered. (That was her usual reply—she was a contented and easy-going child who answered "sure" instead of "yes.")

"Well," I said, "would you like for me to pray, or would you like to pray?" "I'll pray," she answered. Mom, Dad, and chaplain joined hands with the six-year-old patient, and she began to pray for her parents, for Oma and Opa, for her friends, for me, for her cat, for her dog, and basically for the whole world. It was a long, beautiful prayer. We hugged, and I was immediately hooked on my newfound ministry in the children's hospital.

A few months later, I was called to the pediatric intensive care unit. An infection had spread throughout the girl's body, and it had put her into a coma. She now lay dying in her mother's arms. Life support was disconnected, and her little body was shutting down. I went to comfort, only to be comforted by her parents. They would not trade anything for their life with her and all that she had taught them about living and loving. Their daughter truly knew God, and now she was "at home" with Him.

That day I learned an important lesson: Although adults often find it difficult to shut out the busy world to spend time with God, getting to know God remains simple enough that any child can do it. It is merely a choice.

Transition as a Never-Ending Process

Some ministers retire with an expectation that their transition will function as a single point in time, or at most, a slightly longer phase of passage. They expect to emerge from this process as a finished, new product labeled "retiree." While this expectation might ring true for many transitions, it remains a huge fallacy for retirement transition. Instead of seeing it as a point in time, you will discover that retirement transition functions as a never-ending process lasting until death. As physical constraints progressively affect your ministry and social network, you will experience a never-ending process of retirement transition. This is not simply a process of "letting go." It is a never-ending process of partnering with God to refocus yourself, constantly discovering new avenues in which God can use you, and constantly learning new, deeper ways to facilitate communion with God and others.

Thus, if you view retirement transition as a *point in time*, the process breaks down as soon as you need a further lifestyle change. If you view retirement transition as a never-ending process, however, you will finish well, thriving with God's help until your last breath.

Those who fail to retire successfully often fail because their transition never became a lifestyle process of never-ending transition. Ministry couple "D" offer a sad example of this. His discovery that he suffered from a progressive incurable disease forced him to retire. He planned the initial phase of his retirement rather well, and found a large church in which he could minister as an assistant. Although he transitioned into his new ministry extremely well, he failed to adopt retirement transition as an ongoing lifestyle. Therefore, he never planned on altering his ministerial functions as his illness progressed. When his illness reached the point at which he could no longer accomplish the function assigned in the local church, the church dismissed him. Without an alternative plan for further meaningful ministry, he and his wife grew deeply depressed.

Many ministers with chronic diseases find that they constantly need to reinvent their ministry due to the progressive disabling effect of their disease. For them, they barely adjust to their new roles before they need to begin transitioning once again. Unlike other transitions, successful retirement transition requires a choice to adopt transition as a never-ending lifestyle. As a "retired" minister, you will reinvent yourself again and again as you progress through the process of finishing well.

Retirement Insights from Scripture

(Reprinted with permission of Ken Mayo, missionary to Eurasia)

Is a "Call of God" a call for life? In the spring, 1995 issue of *Christian Counseling Today*, in an article entitled "The Calling", Dr. Lee Hardy of Calvin College says, "God does not call a few people out of the world into special religious work, leaving the rest without a calling" (16). Dr. Hardy's statement is consistent with my study of 1 Peter 4:10 and Romans 12:4-21, where the idea of "the call" is to the body of Christ— the Church—in order to build up other believers and help the body to be effective in ministry. Dr. Hardy additionally points out, "A calling does not come from an employer, but from God, who gifts us for specific tasks" (17). The bottom line is that all followers of Christ are "called" into ministry for life.

For most people, a key point of tension about this subject comes because of the historic position of the church to connect "the Call" with an occupation and a location. The notion of a "special calling" comes out of the Protestant Reformation, where one would choose a vocation based on calling, gifts, abilities, and interests. So, for good reason, one can feel a sense of disobedience if she or he leaves the field of calling—be it a missionary who now resides in his passport country or the chaplain who is no longer in the military.

In order to see this in another context, we can look at 1 Corinthians 7:20, ". . . remain in the calling wherein you were called" (NLT). The main idea here is to serve Christ wherever you are. I am beginning to unhook my call from location. Furthermore, this passage helps me see that a calling doesn't come from an employer, be it my mission agency or New Life Fellowship in Tiny Town, Florida. My calling comes from God, who has gifted me for specific tasks and ministry both in the local church and beyond. This helps me also to disconnect my call from an occupation.

Without getting into a long theological discussion about why to retire, I've chosen to look at passages about Old Testament Levites (understood here to include priests within the Levite tribe and other Israelite tribes) as a guide to understanding ministry retirement. For one, they represent a broad ministry group in Scripture with whom someone in Christian ministry can identify. And second, the New Testament is fairly silent when it comes to the subject. The vast majority of the New Testament ministry personages with whom one could identify encountered forced retirement through martyrdom, exile, or imprisonment.

A review of Scripture reveals few instances of the word *retirement*. One of the first occurrences is Num. 8:25, "...but at the age of fifty, they [the Levites] must retire from their regular service and work no longer" (NIV). Although the starting and retirement age for priests varies in the Old Testament, it appears that age was a significant criterion (mentioned seven times in Numbers 4 alone). There is a considerable range of viewpoint about the exact meaning of these age-related rules; however, most agree on a basic point—at a certain age, the Levites were required to stop doing some aspects of their duties and retire.

Having established retirement for Levites at the age of fifty, Moses qualifies this by adding, "They may assist their brothers in performing their duties at the Tent of Meeting, but they themselves must not do the work" (Num. 8:26, NIV). A reasonable understanding of why Moses is given this mandate from the Lord is because of how physically demanding the work was, traipsing through the burning desert, setting up and taking down a huge tent, carrying all the tabernacle articles on their backs, butchering thousands of animals, chopping piles of wood for holy fire, and so on. Not that anything magical happens when we turn fifty, but our physical condition and energy level tell us something significant about when it is time to retire. Could it be that God our Creator knows something about how long we are able to keep working as we did when we were younger?

In order to get a broader biblical understanding on retirement, one has to look at scriptural concepts about retirement rather than for each occurrence of the word "retire." Numbers chapters 3, 4, and 8 enlighten us conceptually about levitical ministry and retirement as it pertains to a more mobile ministry. It seems that during those days there were four broad categories of levitical ministry: 1) guard duty, 2) service in the sanctuary, 3) physical work, and 4) skilled work.

The levitical rules seemed to change over the course of time from Moses until Hezekiah—some thousand or so years. As the rules changed, the roles changed. For example, under the direction of David, the beginning age was lowered to twenty and the retirement age was increased to fifty-five. The Levites were divided into twenty-four different groupings, with each group having a unique assignment to perform. These not so subtle rule changes led to more "hands on" involvement in the sanctuary, such as: 1) liturgical singing and playing of instruments: 2) door keeping; 3) managing the storage facilities and outbuildings; 4) taking care of temple utensils; 5) preparing holy ointments, spices, and baked goods; 6) serving as scribes; and 7) fulfilling administrative duties as judges (see 1 Chron. 6.16-34; 9.22-33; 23.24-32; 26.29-32).

When, under Solomon, a more permanent worship structure was built, the levitical roles David set in place were solidified, and the roles of the twenty-four priestly divisions were expanded to include service as caretakers of the temple in Jerusalem (see 2 Chron. 5.7-14; 8.14-16). A bit later (17:7-9), Jehoshaphat instituted an itinerant band of levitical educators. They were assigned the role of making rounds to all the cities in Judah to offer instruction in Mosaic Law (Torah). Finally, Hezekiah engaged Levites in suspending the rules governing feasts in order for the celebration to continue for seven extra days. By so doing, the Levites expanded their roles to include leading the people in corporate worship and prayers. Hezekiah then reinstituted the twenty-four Davidic priestly divisions, the important role of teaching Mosaic Law in the Temple, and receiving food and material goods for the priests' livelihood. The resulting blessing of these reforms necessitated that the Levites engage in animal husbandry, warehouse work, and financial accounting to oversee the abundant giving for cultic worship (30.21- 31.19).

The significance of this progressive change in levitical functions can be helpful as guidance to those in ministry entering retirement and looking for meaningful ways to continue in their calling. This overview points out how the Levites were somewhat forced into retooling their skill sets as a result of changes in rules and roles over which they had little control. If one is to continue to sense fulfillment in ministry during retirement, one must seek to expand his or her view of what roles one can fill. Once again, this requires a flexible approach to ministry that allows one to release the call from location and occupation.

Along with mandatory retirement, Mosaic guidelines (see Deut. 18:1-2) made no allotment of land for the Levites. During those days it was understood that offerings of various sorts would sustain the Levites and provide their livelihood until they died. This privilege was taken to the extreme by Levites in Hezekiah's days, who were receiving the benefit yet rendering no cultic functions (see 2 Chron. 29.11).

Ministry accountability is necessary if one is to receive compensation. Most churches and financial partners are reluctant to engage in the type of ministry support going on during Old Testament days where Levites were supported until death. Today, the more general expectation is that those in ministry should be supported only until such time as they are no longer able to perform productively.

In bringing these thoughts to a close, I'm almost tempted to say to myself, "I'm not a Levite. This doesn't apply to me." Perhaps, in a strict sense, this is true. However, as I near retirement, these biblical examples help me realize what a significant transition is taking place. This transition calls for openness to new ideas and flexibility at a time in my life when everything in me wants continuity and stability. Most likely, transition into retirement for those Levites turning fifty-five was no different from what you or I will experience. Could it be that they trusted the Lord who called them and whom they worshiped to help them find a way to adjust to change and engage in meaningful ministry? That is what I am purposing to do. What about you?

Personal Reflections on Successful Retirement

1. If successful retirement includes four characteristics: (1) pursuing physical health, (2) pursuing intimacy with God, (3) pursuing social interaction, and (4) pursuing meaningful ministry:

   - What ministers do you know who have retired successfully?
     - —
     - —
     - —

   - Which of the above ministers might serve as your mentor during retirement transition?

   - Of those who retired successfully, what do they say helped them during retirement transition?
     - —
     - —
     - —

   - What ministers do you know who have retired with difficulty?
     - —
     - —
     - —

   - Does the lack of any of the four support legs for successful retirement seem to typify those who failed to retire successfully?

2. What are some of your initial plans to pursue physical health during retirement?

3. What are some of your initial plans to pursue intimacy with God during retirement?

4. What are some of your initial plans for widening your social support network during retirement?

5. What are some of your initial plans for a meaningful ministry during retirement?

6. What are two of your greatest fears about retirement?
   -
   -

7. Change is an external factor that will affect your transition into retirement. What external factors do you expect might affect your transition?

    • How might your roles change?

        –

        –

        –

        –

    • What relationships will you have to leave behind?

        –

        –

        –

        –

    • What routines will likely change?

        –

        –

        –

        –

    • What else will likely change?

        –

        –

        –

        –

8. In contrast to change, transition reflects an internal adjustment of attitudes, and assumptions that will affect your transition into retirement. What internal attitudes and assumptions do you expect might change during your transition?

    •

•

9. There is little reason for you to focus on "letting go" during retirement, except to let go of middle-age behaviors that hinder you from thriving.

    •   What middle-age behaviors might hinder you from thriving during retirement?

        –   Dietary habits:

        –   Relationship deficits:

        –   Exercise habits:

        –   Spiritual growth habits:

        –   Work habits:

        –   Other behaviors and habits:

    •   There is every reason to focus on replacement attitudes and assumptions that will help you thrive during retirement. What replacement habits might counter those listed above?

10. Above, we noted that successful retirees often do not begin to reach their most productive years until they are seniors.

- What are some productive ministries that you would like to pursue during retirement?

  —

  —

  —

  —

- What are some productive activities outside of ministry that you would like to pursue during retirement?

  —

  —

  —

Learning From The Past

1. What are some meaningful ways that you have contributed to the Kingdom of God during you past ministry? Reminisce and list these experiences.

2. During your career, list the times that God unmistakably intervened and caused His will to happen in your life:

3. What are your insights from these prior instances of God's intervention? How will those insights serve you during you retirement transition?

4. How did your family and/or significant others respond or react to your retirement decision?

5. How will they be impacted?

6. What might I do to facilitate their adjustment?

CHAPTER 2

 ## The Involvement Stage

If I rise on the wings of the dawn, if I settle on the far side of the sea, even there your hand will guide me, your right hand will hold me fast (Psalm 139:9-10, NIV).

Retirement transition includes five stages as defined by Dr. David Pollock (reprinted with permission from Interaction International).

Stage	Key Word	Sense of Time
1. Involvement	Settled	Present
2. Leaving	Unsettled	Future oriented, temporary
3. Transition	Chaos	Future
4. Entering	Settling	Future
5. Re-involvement	Engaged	Settled/present

Category	Involvement Stage	Leaving Stage	Transition Stage	Entering Stage	Re-involvement
Social Posture	**Committed** — Responsible, Responsive	**Distancing** — Loosen ties, Relinquish Roles, Disengage	**Chaos** — Must initiate relationship, Isolation, Self-centered	**Superficial** — Observer, Uncertain trust, Exaggerated	**Committed** — Belonging of Involved, Conforming behavior
Social Status	**Belonging** — Part of "In" Group, Reputation, Position	**Celebration** — Attention, Recognition, Farewells, Closures	**Statusless** — Special knowledge without use	**Introducing** — Unknown, Lack structure, Marginal	**Belonging** — Known of Knowing Position
Psychological Experience	**Intimacy** — Confirmed, Secured	**Denial** — Rejection, Resentment, Sadness, Guilt, Anticipation	**Anxiety** — Dissolution of ego, Ambiguity/sacred objects, Grief from loss, Emotional instability	**Vulnerable** — Fearful, Ambivalent, Easily offended	**Intimacy** — Secure, Affirmed

David Pollock's Transition Model

(reprinted with permission from Interaction International. To learn more about Interaction, TCKs, re-entry transitions, or for resources, write Interaction at P.O. Box 863, Wheaton, IL 60189, or www.interactionintl.org).

Involvement (the Pre-retirement stage) represents the stage at which the minister feels fully engaged in ministry prior to considering retirement. In the involvement stage, the minister focuses on the present. For example, most ministers would state that they feel like, "I am engaged in a ministry role for which I am well suited and comfortable. I have a sense of status where people know me and know what I am capable of doing. And, at an emotional level, I'm probably feeling loved, valued and appreciated." Who would want to leave those conditions? However, change happens and some day their future suddenly becomes their present. As Spencer Johnson says in his book, *The Present*, "You create your own present by what you give your attention to today" (2003, p. 40).

Dave Pollock notes that the involvement stage is generally characterized by:

A. Commitment. For ministers who have not yet retired, they usually feel a sense of commitment and responsibility in their assignment. Individuals belong to their work team, and feel committed to their work.

B. Belonging. Ministers have a job position, know what to do, and are recognized for their role, both by their work team as well as other churches.

C. Intimacy. Ministers feel known and accepted not only for the work that they accomplish but also for their unique personality characteristics and personal lifestyle behaviors.

The Involvement Stage ends when the minister discovers that it is time to seriously consider retirement. Often, a minister feels almost embarrassed by peers who ask, "Isn't it time for you to retire?" Although the minister still offers wide-ranging skills, he or she may feel prompted by guilt to retire. Affected by well-meaning but somewhat insensitive peers, some ministers retire too early. Many ministers feel unsure about when to retire (i.e., when to end the involvement stage).

Determining When to Retire: Two Key Criteria

You may decide to retire when you reach the age at which you qualify to receive Social Security income. However, ministers are not always required to retire at any particular "retirement age" or when they first become eligible to receive Social Security. In many non-western cultures, older ministers are often highly valued for their knowledge, experience, and relationships. However, most organizations will conduct an annual review of each retirement eligible minister to determine two things:

1. Is the minister still productive in his or her ministry?
2. Does the minister retain an excellent relationship with team-members, parishioners and other local churches?

Generally speaking, ministers who reach "retirement age" are not asked to retire because of poor health—they are asked to retire only if their health makes them non-productive. Also, they are not asked to retire because of the type of ministry they are doing—they are only asked to retire if that ministry is a non-productive ministry. They are not even asked to retire because they can't raise an adequate church or personal budget—they are asked to retire only if they let their budget affect their personal or church productivity. Usually, they can continue with a lower budget if they are able and wish to provide personal funds to stay active and productive. When a minster reaches retirement age, if he or she remains only marginally productive or retains poor relationships with other coworkers or other local workers, he or she will be required to retire. Therefore, it is vital throughout one's career to pay greater attention to these two evidences of effective ministry.

Although past retirement age, one minister was recently asked to speak at a large youth conference. As he finished speaking, a young man raised his hand to ask the following question: "If you could go back and change any one thing in your past, what would you change?" After a brief moment, the missionary replied, "Unfortunately, no one can go back and undo the past. However, if I could, I would be more careful to build and maintain good relationships with all those with whom I worked and associated." To his amazement, the young people began to stand and clap their hands. It seems that they were able to comprehend what some ministers fail to understand until it is too late: *good relationships are vital for effective ministry.*

These same two criteria (productivity and relationship) also indicate when it is appropriate to fire a minister. That is, an individual should not retain his or her ministerial position if he or she becomes unproductive or destroys relationships, at any age.

Each of us will eventually grow less productive due to health concerns or lack of energy. When that happens (and not *if* that happens) it is time to retire.

Thus, age remains an inappropriate factor to determine if it is time to retire. Productivity and relationships are key factors to consider, and need to be considered at every age.

Since the decision to retire primarily depends on personal choices, consider the following change equation developed by Dr. Russ Rogers (DePaul University professor and organizational psychologist).

Change = $\underline{F}$uture + $\underline{S}$teps > Cost

Note: This is not an actual equation, but offers a way to better understand the likelihood of change. If F or S equals zero, then the likelihood of change greatly diminishes.

In order to envision that desired *Future*, you may want to ask yourself the following:

- What are my reasons for serving the body of Christ?

- What are my needs and obligations for serving the body of Christ?

- What ministries do I feel enthusiastic about?

- What are some ways I can serve the body of Christ?

- Where can my specific abilities, gifts and experience be used?

- In order to identify some first known *Steps*, you may want to consider the following:

- Evaluate what you need to do now to position yourself for your next ministry.

- Determine what new training you need for that ministry.

- Find other people engaged in the type of ministry to which you would like to transition—obtain their input to identify your first steps toward that ministry.

- Seek guidance from those in leadership such as a supervisor or a trusted pastor friend.

God has called each minister to proclaim the gospel message. This must always be done in a spirit of serving and encouraging others. To illustrate His answer to the question, "Who is the greatest in the kingdom of God?" Jesus used a child. May those who work with us see us as children of God, proclaiming the gospel in a spirit of love and respect for others. May all those with whom we work speak well of us, and may they encourage us to continue finishing well until Christ comes or calls us home.

CHAPTER 3

The
Leaving
Stage

I can't change the direction of the wind, but I can adjust my sails to always reach my destination.—Jimmy Dean

The leaving stage is characterized by an emotional reaction to the individual's impending retirement.

The leaving stage is mastered by building a retirement plan that addresses the primary concerns of the leaving stage:

1. New ministry goals
2. Financial security goals
3. Academic goals

For the minister retiring successfully, this stage usually precedes physically leaving his or her assignment by at least two years, depending on how much the minister needs to prepare for retirement. That is, the leaving stage initiates well before the minister physically leaves his or her assignment. For many North American ministers, this stage initiates between age sixty-four to sixty-six due to social security considerations and persists until the minister physically transitions to the next assignment. Generally, the retirement transition grows easier as the minister develops an increasingly thorough and complete retirement plan.

The Emotional Reaction of Distancing

The *Leaving Stage* is the first stage at which the minister usually experiences an emotional response to retirement transition. If the emotional reaction is not processed adequately, the minister (especially a missionary or chaplain) may easily face stress that exceeds his or her coping capacity. Please take time to contemplate and, more importantly, discuss the common emotional reactions listed below.

The preparatory responses for "Leaving" are normal emotional responses that lessen the pain of separation. In the military, individuals in this stage are commonly called "FIGMO." FIGMO is an acrostic that means, "Finally I Got My Orders (orders to move to a new job)." Most co-workers immediately notice that the FIGMO individual starts to disengage emotionally from work and from co-workers. Since most ministers feel a very strong emotional tie to a God-given ministerial call, this normal emotional response usually affects the retiring minister much more than those in the military or anywhere else. Ministers often feel quite guilty for feeling disengaged (feeling FIGMO) during their final year or two. However, this is a normal and almost unavoidable emotional response. Rather than languishing in guilt, it is more appropriate to use the leaving stage to prepare for retirement. Preparation for retirement is, itself, a full-time job that begins with preparation for leaving.

A Loosening of Relationship Ties

Distancing includes a loosening of relationship ties in preparation for leaving. Frequently, even the closest of friends will notice a cooling in their friendship. This is normal. However, the individual in the leaving stage sometimes even develops deep anger toward those who were formerly loved. Generally, the stronger the love, the more susceptible the individual becomes to employing anger and "bridge-burning" to lessen the pain of leaving. With a close emotional bond still intact, a minister will certainly feel intense grief after separation. Take notice when you feel anger toward those whom you will leave behind. Anger represents a normal but inappropriate feeling when used simply to lessen the grief of leaving. An unnamed missionary recently retired with relative emotional ease, but only after destroying all his former relationships. By the time he destroyed all his formerly close relationships, he was barely able to retire before being told to resign.

As an individual begins to disengage in the leaving stage, stress increases. You may experience a variety of emotional responses including excitement, a sense of loss, relief, anxiety, and uncertainty. The following list may help you identify and work through some thoughts and feelings associated with moving out of this stage. Explicitly write out your steps and response for the following:

- Describe specifically what is changing.

- Identify who is losing what (Accept the reality and importance of non-material losses such as a relationship).

- Remind yourself not to feel surprised by overreaction. To what could you overreact?

- Expect and accept the signs of grieving. What will you grieve?

- Define what is over and what isn't.

- Mark when things actually end, such as the last time you will visit a certain church.

- Treat the past with respect—what do you now find is important from your past life, and what now looks less important?

- Think about what you will take with you into the next phase—what is continuing?

- Don't drag endings out; plan them carefully and bring them to closure. What do you need to end?

Disengaging From Prior Ministry and the Culture

Distancing includes disengaging from prior ministry and the culture. Some ministers in the leaving stage disengage from ministry prematurely—even while they can still make a meaningful impact. It seems difficult to maintain focus on one's prior ministry when needing to prepare for a new retirement ministry. Some peers accused a minister in the leaving stage of forgetfulness and senility, when in fact he simply felt overwhelmed and preoccupied with trying to prepare for his new retirement ministry. Try scheduling specific periods of the day to focus on each ministry separately. Leave yourself "to do" notes that keep you focused on your prior ministry. While you need to prepare for a new ministry, resist the tendency to disengage prematurely from a long-time ministry.

Some ministers in the leaving stage want to prematurely relinquish their responsibilities even while they remain able to lead and minister. For instance, some individuals stop caring for their home, auto, and other organizationally owned facilities even while they can still function as a minister. Reflect honestly and openly about any desire to relinquish responsibilities during this stage. It is appropriate to prepare for a new ministry in retirement, but inappropriate to relinquish responsibility to those unprepared and unsuspecting.

Denial

When the retirement transition initiates earlier than expected, some individuals simply refuse to accept their impending retirement. Unable to accept the reality, they deny the need to plan. Denial usually happens when a minister refuses to:

- acknowledge sadness over a loss

- deal with guilt and regrets from the past

- plan for the upcoming retirement transition.

Rejection

A minister in the leaving stage often feels rejected when others begin to leave him or her out of their planning. The minister may feel unvalued or worthlessness. It is a false belief because—if rationally questioned—most ministers would want their ministries to continue without their continued planning and support. Angry at those who leave him or her out of the planning and decision process, the minister in the leaving stage sometimes lashes out in anger at colleagues. Potential references for future ministry are destroyed, not to mention the demise of close friendships.

Celebration and Farewells

Formal retirement rituals sometimes provide few positive memories for the retiree. Such rituals usually include advanced announcements of a party, speeches by supervisors, a gift (often an all-purpose gift that seems almost meaningless to the retiree), food, and the religious equivalent of a ceremonial toast (usually in the form of a ceremonial prayer). Completing the following informal activities remain critical to the process of leaving and making good adjustments:

- Say goodbye to people in ways appropriate to the culture.

- Say goodbye to places. This is particularly important for missionaries and chaplains who may feel unable to return at a later date.

- Take care of unfinished business and unresolved interpersonal conflicts. Plan very intentionally to mend hurting relationships and receive/grant forgiveness.

- Reaffirm relationships. Take time to remember the positives and validate your friends for their contribution to you and your ministry.

Whatever you do, don't retire before repairing your hurting relationships. The old relationship patterns will repeat themselves if you fail to address them now.

Although the formal retirement rituals may retain little meaning, the informal rituals remain extremely meaningful. Since a retirement ceremony is YOUR party, consider planning it much like you might plan you own wedding. Few others know how to make the farewell more meaningful than you can. If no one else plans your retirement party, plan your own and invite only those whom you want. If you are leaving a country in which there are no other ministers, you may want to host two parties: one in your adopted country for local personnel, and another in your country of origin or at your area/regional retreat. Regardless of who is planning the party, Savishinsky, in *Breaking the Watch: The Meaning of Retirement in America* (2000) suggests that you have your say in these ways:

- developing the guest list, including participation by family and relatives;

- being recognized as an individual, not within a group of other retirees;

- developing a "memory" book in which guests can write about the retiree;

- choosing your gift—one that is tailored to your interests as the retiree; and

- acknowledging truthfully (to yourself and to all your team members) how you feel about your past career.

  - What are you sad to leave behind?

  - What are you glad to leave behind?

  - How can you appropriately point out what the organization needs, most?

Developing Sections 1, 2, and 3 of Your Retirement Plan

George Elliot said, "It's never too late to be who you might have been." Retirement is a great time to become more than you are. In *How to Retire Happy, Wild, and Free,* Ernie Zelinski notes, "Being on purpose is easy, if you have one" (2005, 50). Since retirement can easily continue for up to one-fourth of one's lifetime, plan your goals purposefully. Milton Mayer said, "What can a man do who doesn't know what to do?"

The retirement transition process stresses almost every minister, and especially missionaries and chaplains. Psychologist Richard Lazarus notes (2006), "It is the capacity to cope that converts stress into challenge. Stress by itself is not pathogenic; it becomes pathogenic only when stress exceeds coping resources." Prior to planning, stress can easily exceed coping resources. When stress exceeds our coping resources for an extended time period, it grows pathogenic, even resulting in burnout and depression. However, the planning process usually brings the stress level back into a normal range.

A Concrete Retirement Plan

Structure and schedule act as the primary antidotes to the chaos and stress of leaving and transition. Structure develops as the minister builds specific personal plans across all the domains of a healthy life.

Plan with three purposes in mind:

First and most importantly, plan for retirement while you still feel well and remain free from the effect of any crisis. Successful retirement planning usually requires a considerable amount of time—two to three years. However, some individuals begin retirement planning only after a crisis or illness forces them into an earlier than expected retirement. They fail to productively negotiate numerous life-changing retirement decisions because illness reduces their energy, concentration and clarity while simultaneously increasing their tendency to base decisions on emotions instead of rational reasoning. Therefore, make your retirement decisions based on wellness, not on illness or other crises. Developing a retirement plan while you still feel well ensures that you define your own retirement instead of letting an illness define your retirement.

If you develop an illness prior to the transition process, try to obtain inputs from multiple sources before making decisions about ministerial functions and geographical relocation. Even minor illness predisposes one to make emotion-based decisions instead of rational decisions. Seek counsel from multiple sources if you suffer from any illness.

Second, adjust to unexpected changes (such as illness) by referencing and updating your existing plan as the unexpected events and crises occur. Don't discard your existing plan due to an unexpected crisis. Simply update it.

Third, periodically update your plan on a pre-determined schedule (at least every two years) to account for new opportunities.

During the leaving stage, the prospective retiree's Retirement Plan should meet three needs:

1. A plan for a new and better ministry
2. A plan for financial security
3. A plan for academic growth

Retirement Plan Section 1:
A Change in Ministry

What makes life meaningful and purposeful for a minister? Of all the tasks and efforts in which minister's endeavor, which really matter? For most of us, ministry provides one of the primary purposes for being. Robert Emmons, a professor of psychology at the University of California at Davis, states (1999, 107),

> Personal strivings in life can become sanctified or imbued with a sense of the holy. As a consequence, they are likely to be appraised differently than are secularized strivings. When work is seen as a calling rather than a job, or as an opportunity to serve God, work-related strivings take on new significance.

Ministers are inherently goal oriented—toward worldwide ministry. Everything about the minister's life gets structured around his or

> *For a minister facing retirement, the most significant danger is not the loss of a future income, but the loss of a psychological future— the loss of one's hope to make specific future contributions toward the Kingdom of God.*

her "call" to ministry. Although few ministers pursue a goal to be happy, their happiness usually results from their relationship with God and from their other ministry relationships. "Whereas it is possible for a life to be imbued with significance yet devoid of happiness, (e.g., the lives of some religious martyrs), it is impossible for long-term happiness to occur in a life devoid of meaning" (Emmons, 1999, 138). Thus, when a minister's ability to minister gets firmly blocked or taken away by retirement, he or she loses one of the major purposes in life, and physical and emotional health subsequently falters. For the retired minister, retirement can easily initiate a career of the "roleless role" (Veroff & Veroff, 1980). It may seem like the first time that you no longer fill the role as teacher, preacher, speaker, evangelizer, counselor, writer, leader, missionary, or chaplain. Without a role as a minister, what are you to do?

The average retirement age minister possesses such a wide diversity of talents and so much cultural flexibility that he or she can accomplish many more roles than younger ministers. Very few retirement age ministers lack talent and ability. However, some find difficulty in developing a pathway to use their talent and abilities in a new ministry role.

Some ministers make few or no plans for pursuing a ministry after retirement. Rev. Duel Tanner, an eighty-nine year old "retired" minister, when asked what single piece of advice he would give to ministers entering retirement, said, "Don't retire! Simply change the focus of your ministry to a new focus that is appropriate to your new culture." He went on to say, "Too many ministers retire to a life that is devoid of ministry even though they still feel a call to ministry. God's call doesn't end simply because a minister reaches retirement age. Pray, pray, pray for insight and guidance." To illustrate this point, Rev. Tanner pointed out that during the two years following his eighty-seventh birthday, he preached more than sixty times and continued to encourage younger ministers during the sectional meetings of the churches in his area.

Why plan? For three reasons:

First, retirement age ministers without meaningful retirement plans grow increasingly susceptible to major illness and death within the first six years following retirement. This single factor sets ministerial retirement transition apart from almost all other transitions. Even though re-entry transition, ministry transition, geographical transition, and marital transition seem difficult, they rarely result in illness and death.

Without adequate retirement transition planning, a minister can expect the loss of his or her ministerial functions, self-image, social relationships, spiritual relationships, hope, future dreams, and emotional health. The emotional turmoil may grow so destructive that illness and death turn into reality. Plan as though your life depends on it—it may.

Second, retirement planning results in hopeful thinking and happiness. Planning helps a minister to control his or her future and replaces feelings of insecurity and anxiety with hope. Retirees with purpose and plans can transition easier and live a happier life. Those who plan little are usually successful—at doing little.

Regardless of your financial or medical status, as a minister facing retirement, your most significant issue is—

"What will I do with the rest of my life?"

Third, and most importantly, God calls individuals into ministry *for life.* Therefore, most ministers expect to minister for as long as they live. It's an honor and a joy to serve God and others. A thriving minister never retires totally from ministry; we merely shift horizontally to another means of ministry.

Frequently, the secular retiree's most important retirement issue is, "How much money will I take with me into retirement?" The retirement age minister can also adopt this same viewpoint, and that may reflect the degree to which a minister syncretizes his or her religious values with secular culture. However, the most important question facing a retirement age minister remains the same question that he or she faced upon deciding to enter the ministry, "What will I do with the rest of my life?" This singular issue defines a minister's retirement transition as a much more significant transition than any other life transition. Until the retirement age minister can adequately answer this question, he or she will fail to retire successfully regardless of his or her financial status. When you first decided to enter ministry, your prospective financial income probably played a minor role in the decision process. Likewise, your prospective social security income and other financial income are not the most important issues as you transition into retirement.

What are some potential new ministry goals following retirement? How will you balance your retirement freedom with the responsibility of your call to ministry? What legacy would you like to leave? When considering potential new ministry goals, note the following five categories:

a. What types of ministry activities do you enjoy or dislike?

To help you evaluate the types of ministry activities that you might enjoy or want to avoid, please log onto the following website: http://www.five-factor.com (please note the – symbol between the words "five" and "factor") and complete the personality assessment. Your printouts will include the five factor model (FFM) scores and 22 facet scores. Based on these scores, additional printouts are computed for the fruit of the Spirit, motivational gifts of the Spirit, team potentials, behavior styles, and occupational interests. *Transforming Personality: Spiritual Formation and the Five Factor Model* (see inside flap of the front cover of this book for details to obtain this book) will help you to better understand your five factor printouts and the associated charts.

The FFM personality assessment scores are shown in units of standard deviation, a unit of measure in which "0" represents the average for a people group such as the North American population. For personality assessments, values less than ½ standard deviations from the norm (0) are generally considered meaningless differences. However, differences over ½ standard deviations increasingly cause behavior to deviate from the norm. As a rule of thumb, consider a ½ standard deviation of difference as a slight difference, a 1 standard deviation of difference as a moderate difference, a 2 standard deviation difference as a major difference, and a 3 standard deviation difference as a massive difference.

Your FFM personality scores indicate your general preferences for various types of work. When accessing http://www.five-factor.com, make sure to obtain the complete list of available printouts. The complete list will include charts showing your vocational interests and ministry interests (see samples in Figures 2 and 3, below).

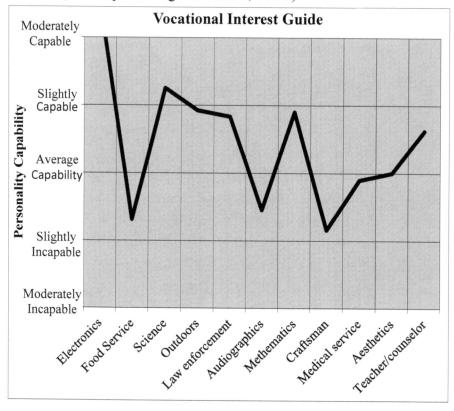

Figure 2: Sample Printout of Vocational Interests

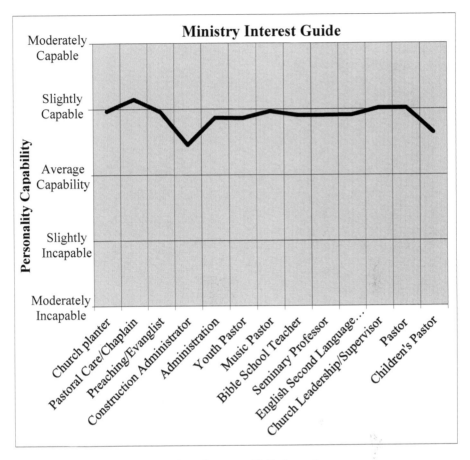

Figure 3: Sample Printout of Ministry Interests

Reflecting on your occupational and ministry printouts from http://www.five-factor.com, what vocational roles and ministry roles are enhanced by your personality traits?

-
-
-
-

What ministry roles and job functions should you try to avoid?

-
-
-
-
-

What made your previous ministry activities enjoyable, (e.g. power, control, leadership, autonomy, clear direction, creativity, team relationships, meaningfulness, service, feedback, recognition, acceptance, etc.)?

Obtain help from your spouse or friends to develop a complete list of previous ministry activities that you enjoyed along with the reasons why you enjoyed them.

-
-
-
-
-

What types of ministries would you like to do that you never got around to doing?

-
-
-
-

-

b. During your ministry, what kinds of activities have you accomplished best, regardless of whether you enjoyed them or not?

Most ministers, through necessity, develop skills for activities that they dislike. At what activities are you adept, even though you do not enjoy doing them? Reminisce for a moment about those activities and events.

-

-

-

-

c. Has God called you to perform specific tasks?

Note that God called the prophet Jonah to perform specific tasks that he disliked. Your ministry may require activities that you dislike, too. Please note that for some individuals, finding their niche of ministry is often more about them than about God. We invite you to consider that you are merely one of millions of players in God's drama about humankind. So, we invite you to consider that His plan may consider other factors that are more important than your particular likes and dislikes. Has God called you to do something specifically? Has He put you in a place that you can contribute something to His kingdom that remains outside of your comfort zone? Please list these specific callings or special opportunities God has provided.

-

-

-

-

-

d. What legacy do you want to leave when you die?

How do you want people to think of your life when they remember you?

-

-

-

-

-

e. Based on the above four categories (a through d), what types of potential ministry might you pursue after retirement?

(Please list potential ministry areas without judging if they are possible, and without considering how to develop the skills needed. This is simply a brainstorming list.)

-

-

-

-

-

Retirement Plan Section 2: Financial Security

Please note that your financial security will vary greatly depending on the country in which you retire. While this book presents some of the considerations relevant to those who retire in the USA, we readily acknowledge that the majority of worldwide ministers retire in countries outside the USA. This book cannot address the unique financial considerations relevant to each country.

For ministers who plan to retire in the USA, log onto http://www.socialsecurity.gov/ no later than age 65 for the latest information about filing for social security. Most large cities in the USA include a social security office in which citizens can sign up for social security benefits. Most U.S. consulates also employ a retirement specialist who will assist missionaries and expatriates in signing up for Social Security benefits.

Upon becoming eligible to receive social security, most ministers who remain employed in their job will transition to a status we call, "retirement eligible." This means that they will receive dual incomes—a retirement income from the Social Security Administration as well as an income from their normal ministry. If both husband and wife qualify to receive social security, married individuals will receive two social security incomes in addition to their normal income. Some "retirement eligible" ministers can live comfortably solely on their social security income. Fortunately, some "retirement eligible" ministers retain an option to invest their ministerial salary into a Rabbi Trust. Funds placed in a Rabbi Trust can be withdrawn, without taxation, for house payments. Please contact your church agency finance office if you would like to set up a Rabbi Trust. Some retired-active ministers save hundreds of thousands of tax-free dollars by doing this. Specific questions about the

Rabbi Trust can be answered by the AG Financial Services Group, Springfield, Missouri (agfsg@agfsg.org).

Social Security in the United States

The Social Security Administration sends each person age 25 years and older a copy of their earnings statements each year. Upon receipt, compare this statement to your records to check for errors. Report any errors to the Social Security Administration. Please log onto www.ssa.gov/retire to check the Social Security Administration's on-line quick calculator for estimated Social Security earnings based on your age and current earnings. If you reside in the USA, you can check on your Social Security payments and future benefits by calling 1-800-772-1213. The SSA-7004 form is also available on line at www.ssa.gov.online. Although the Social Security Administration will send earnings reports each year, you may not receive the documents if you live at a foreign address. To ask for a copy, contact the Social Security Office by mail at:

Social Security Administration
Office of Public Inquiries
6401 Security Boulevard, Windsor Park Building
Baltimore, MD 21235

Filing For Social Security Benefits

If you live outside the USA, contact your local Social Security office or the American Embassy six months before you want to start receiving Social Security benefits. They will inform you of current developments and instructions. At some embassies you cannot file for Social Security. If you live outside the USA, apply for Social Security and/or Medicare at:

Social Security Administration

Office of International Programs
PO Box 17775
Baltimore, MD 21235-7775

(Write to this address expressing your desire to apply for Medicare and/or Social Security. Indicate whether you are a U.S. citizen and ask for forms or go online at www.ssa.gov/international)

From within the USA, file for benefits by phone, online, or in person at a Social Security office at least three months before you want to begin receiving monthly benefits. The toll-free Social Security Administration number is 1-800-772-1213.

You can apply for Social Security and/or Medicare. As a self-employed person, apply for Medicare at least three months before you want to begin receiving Medicare but no later than age 65.

There is a penalty for applying for Medicare after age 65.

The Social Security Administration indicates that interested persons can apply for Social Security online at www.socialsecurity.gov. From this site, you can apply for retirement benefits or spouse benefits.

Please note that the online social security application does not work from foreign countries.

Information commonly needed when you apply:

- Your Social Security number
- Your birth certificate (if you don't have a birth certificate, you can get one from the State where you were born.
- Your W-2 forms or self-employment tax return for last year
- Your military discharge papers if you had military service

- Your spouse's birth certificate and Social Security number if he or she is applying for benefits

- Children's birth certificates and Social Security numbers, if they're applying for children's benefits

- Proof of U.S. citizenship or lawful alien status if you (or a spouse or child applying for benefits) were not born in the U.S.

- The name of your bank and your account number so your benefits can be directly deposited into your account.

The Social Security office will need original documents or copies certified by the issuing office. Mail or bring them to a Social Security office.

Delayed Retirement Income

Some people wait several years past normal retirement age to begin drawing Social Security benefits. To delay payments makes the monthly payments somewhat larger. Relatively few people delay receiving Social Security past their full retirement age, but the tax advantages and increased benefits sometimes may seem more beneficial than current benefits. However, if you die before you receive any benefits, the benefits you could have obtained are lost. Your Social Security representative should be able to tell you what is most advantageous for you.

An Important Point:
Even if you decide to delay your retirement, make sure to sign up for Medicare at age 65.

If you decide to delay your benefits until after age 65, you should still apply for Medicare benefits within three months of your 65th birthday. If you wait longer, your Medicare medical insurance (Part B) and prescription drug coverage (Part D) may cost you more money. The delay may increase the benefit for the retired worker, but not for the spouse. After age 70, there is no increase in the benefits, even when benefits are delayed.

The allowable earned income that will not affect your Social Security benefits changes each year. Log onto www.socialsecurity.gov/ to obtain the latest information. To avoid penalty in your Social Security checks at a later date, be sure to estimate your earnings for the year of retirement as accurately as possible.

Social Security Full Retirement and Reductions by Age

If you qualify for Social Security, no matter what your full retirement age, you may start receiving benefits as early as age 62. However, benefits are reduced for each month you retire below full retirement age. Log onto http://www.socialsecurity.gov/ to determine the reduction that applies to you.

As a general rule, early retirement will give you about the same total Social Security benefits over your lifetime, but in smaller amounts to take into account the longer period you will receive them.

There are disadvantages and advantages to taking your benefit before your full retirement age. The advantage is that you collect benefits for a longer period of time. The disadvantage is that your benefit is permanently reduced. Each person's situation is different and your Social Security office will help you decide when to begin your benefits.

Social Security: Not Just a Retirement Check.

For most people, Social Security merely provides retirement benefits. But Social Security pays a lot more than just retirement benefits. The program consists of two funds: the Old-Age and Survivors Insurance Trust Fund (OASI) and the Disability Insurance Trust Fund (DI). With this money, the following workers receive monthly benefits:

- Workers who have not yet reached retirement age but are so disabled that they cannot be gainfully employed.

- Spouses (age 62 or older) of retired disabled workers.

- Widows or widowers (age 60 or older) of deceased workers, or disabled widows or widowers (age 50 to 59) of deceased workers.

- Children of retired, disabled, or deceased workers, up to age 18 and high school graduation.

- Dependent parents (age 62 or older) of deceased workers.

- Social Security also pays a lump-sum benefit to surviving spouses or dependent children upon the death of an insured worker or retiree.

An optional supplementary medical insurance program known as Part B Medicare provides additional coverage for physical and surgical services, X-rays, ambulance fees, outpatient services, and other expenses. Apply for both Parts A & B at age 65. Even if Medicare is not in place at age 65, your agency medical insurance can usually act as a Medicare supplement for medical costs outside the USA.

Social Security Web Page "For Women"

Recognizing the special importance of Social Security to women and the need for women to obtain timely, accurate information about their rights to benefits under the program, the Social Security Administration (SSA) provides a website that describes the basic Social Security program information on retirement, survivors, disability, and Supplemental Security Income benefits pertinent to women.

Larry Massanari, Acting Commissioner of Social Security, said, "The Social Security program treats all workers—men and women—exactly the same. But because of different life experiences, the real world results are different. As a group, women live longer than men, earn less, and rely on Social Security for most of their retirement income. They need to know what the program means to them in their particular circumstances."

"For Women," www.ssa.gov/women, provides links to basic information throughout SSA's official Web site—Social Security Online—that can be relevant to women at different stages in their life. The links are grouped in logical categories to coincide with the various life events affecting women:

- Working women
- Beneficiary
- Bride
- Widow
- New mother
- Divorced spouse
- Caregiver

The website at www.ssa.gov/women also provides links to other federal agency websites containing information of interest to women, such as the Department of Labor's "Women's Bureau," the Department of Health and Human Service's "Women's Health," and the White House's "Federal Programs and Resources for Women and Families."

Since November, 2000, interested persons can apply for Social Security retirement benefits online at www.ssa.gov, the official Web site for the Social Security Administration. By completing one application, an individual can now apply for his or her own retirement benefit, or a spouse's benefit or, if eligible for both, his or her own retirement benefit plus their benefit as the spouse of a retired worker.

While both men and women can apply for Social Security spouse's benefits online, the fact remains that more women than men qualify for a Social Security benefit as the spouse of a retired worker. Approximately 700,000 people apply for spouse's benefits annually; over 90 percent of them are women.

New Facts

Did you know that more than 46 million people get benefits from Social Security? This and other statistics can be found in an annual chart-book, "Fast Facts And Figures." The online version of is available at http://www.socialsecurity.gov/policy/. If you are deaf or hard of hearing, call the toll-free TTY number, 1.800.325.0778, between 7:00 AM and 7:00 PM Monday through Friday.

> *Don't delay your retirement just because you don't have*
> *all the documents needed – the people in your local social*
> *security office will help you.*

What should I remember to do after I retire? Remember to tell the Social Security Office whenever there's any change in your life circumstance that affects your benefits. For example, they should be notified if you:

- Move

- Marry or divorce

- Change your name

- Learn your estimated earnings will change

- Change your Direct Deposit accounts

- Adopt a child

- Are no longer caring for a child who receives benefits

- Are a non-citizen and your status changes

- Start getting a pension from work not covered by Social Security

- Get both Social Security and Railroad Retirement benefits

- Leave the United States for more than 30 days

- Become unable to manage your funds

- Are convicted of a criminal offense

- Die

You can find more information about what to do when any of these changes happen, and answers to most of your retirement questions, in, "Retirement Benefits," SSA Publication Number 05-10035.

Retirement Plan Section 3: Academic Growth

When I (Nathan) planned to retire from working for the Air Force, I spent four years taking new educational courses, all prior to resigning. What initially stimulated high anxiety resulted in progressively lower anxiety as I prepared fully for a new ministry and a new lifestyle. The success of the transition depended on four years of detailed plans and education. As you plan for retirement, what new academic goals are needed to support your new ministry?

Please note that many state and community colleges offer free or significantly reduced tuition for seniors. Dr. Joseph Castleberry, president of Northwest University, also served as a missionary to Ecuador. He makes the following observation about possibilities for the "celebration stage" of life:

> Most people do not associate what I call the "celebration phase" with higher education. Still, the trend in recent years shows older people returning to college and seminary in huge numbers. For some, retirement offers the freedom of schedule that allows them to dedicate themselves to areas of learning and creativity long left unattended, often to their great frustration. Some have unfinished business in terms of their life's accomplishments that only an advanced degree will complete. Others desire to achieve the academic qualifications that will formally certify their significant experience and aid them in investing in younger people through teaching. Every year, we welcome retired people who enter seminary with enthusiasm and excitement about the learning that awaits them.
>
> No matter what age or phase of ministry a particular student may be in, seminary and formal education can play a crucial role in providing them with tools that will take them to a new level of professionalism. Just as important, seminary study occurs in the context of deep commitment to the presence and anointing of the Holy Spirit, whom Jesus desires to pour out on the young and the old, on men and women, and on people of diverse racial and ethnic backgrounds and walks of life.

- What courses do you need to transition into a new ministry?

- What are the first three steps toward starting these courses?

- What might slow me down or stop me from taking these courses?

- What are some alternative pathways to reach my goal?

Reflection:

1. What are at least five things I need to "let go of"? And, what are some things that may temporarily ease or help to replace these losses (i.e., a functional substitute)?

2. What things do I need to acknowledge as being over, closed, or simply no longer in my future?

3. As you look back on your entire ministry career, what do you wish you could do differently (physical, emotional, relational, etc.) if you could do it over again?

4. Are there any relationship or interpersonal issues that remain after all my years of service? If so, with whom do I need to repair a relationship, and how will I repair those relationships?

5. Who do I need to forgive before starting a new stage of life?

6. To whom do I need to say farewell? How can I say farewell to them?

7. To what places do I need to say farewell? How can I say farewell to those places?

8. To what things and objects do I need to say farewell?

9. What things do I need to bring with me as a memento of my career?

10. What has been my most frustrating experience, situation, or anticipation about leaving?

11. How is retirement a difficult transition for me?

12. What has caused me to "fret" or feel anxious about leaving?

13. What new values am I bringing into retirement that I didn't have before I became a minister?

14. Am I starting to "lean away" from others or job responsibilities?

15. Am I "leaning away" sooner than appropriate?

16. Do I feel as if others have started, too early, to leave me out of planning future team activities? What responsibilities do I need to start backing away from and letting others assume?

17. Do I have a hand in planning my retirement celebration? If not, who do I need to talk to about this?

18. Who do I need to affirm before I retire? Please list each individual who has contributed to your life and ministry, and how you will affirm them.

19. How will I acknowledge truthfully (to myself and to all my team members) how I feel about my ministerial career? As I prepare for my retirement party, how can I point out the organization's fallacies?

CHAPTER 4

The

Transition

Stage

Life is pleasant. Death is peaceful. It's the transition that's troublesome.—Isaac Asimov

The transition stage generally initiates on one's first day of retirement, and commonly persists for several weeks to several years. This stage ends as one initiates a new retirement ministry and starts to implement his or her newly planned retirement lifestyle. If you planned well enough to transition quickly and almost seamlessly into a new ministry, this stage seems short, lasting only a few weeks. If you fail to develop a retirement plan, including plans for a ministry into which you can transition, this stage may last for many years.

Some ministers feel surprised to find themselves going through the transition stage a second or third time, many years after they initially retire. Transition remains a recurrent stage through which each retiree passes again and again. Change happens—the environment around us changes, we develop new skills and relationships, and our body ages. Because we cannot stop the world or our bodies from changing, we get to experience the transition stage again and again. For the retired minister, more than any secular retiree, we continually readjust our ministerial roles, attitudes, and assumptions to match the change. Because ministers feel called to ministry for a lifetime, they get to experience change more than a secular retiree. Feelings of chaos, worthlessness, ambiguity, anxiety, and grief generally characterize the transition stage.

The Normal Emotions of Transition

Chaos

A lack of schedule, a lack of structure, and exaggeration of problems stimulate feelings of chaos during the transition stage. Almost every part of one's life seems in transition. Check below if you currently experience any of these common feelings:

☐ Nobody seems to care   ☐ Irritation
☐ Decisions are hard to make   ☐ Anger
☐ Bewilderment   ☐ Disillusionment
☐ Frustration   ☐ Too materialistic
☐ Being "out of step" with   ☐ Anxiety
    current values

Feelings of chaos typically result from reverse culture shock coupled with generation shock and self-esteem shock. Don't most ministers (especially missionaries and chaplains) long for the day when they return to their home town and get whisked off as the stars of their home church? Don't they dream of their favorite home-town restaurants, supermarkets, and cook-outs with family and friends?

In reality, many missionaries and chaplains (as well as other ministers) retire and find themselves feeling like misfits, particularly in their home church. They feel paralyzed in their home church because they no longer fill a ministry role. When they moved to a new church assignment or returned as a missionary on furlough, the church received them in triumph. When they return for retirement, they are usually not received at all, or at best, received as one who is "finished." It seems that they retain no further value. In most cultures overseas, retirement age ministers remain highly esteemed for the wisdom that accompanies their age. When North American ministers retire, the church often views them as outdated, technologically inept, "has-beens."

Missionaries deal with culture shock and study it thoroughly. They learn that the cultural cues used in their home country no longer work in the second country, and they acquire special skills that help them cope and adapt. How, then, can it feel so difficult to enter a life of retirement? First, the minister has transitioned into an entirely new person. "In fundamental ways, [being a minister or] living abroad for extended periods of time changes people," says Carolyn M. Fontaine in *Cross Cultural Reentry*. Even prolonged stateside ministry changes most ministers in profound says. Ministers leave affluent alternative vocations and learn one or two languages, live in culturally different cities, and hike through a maze of transitions. They may have lived in a crowded, noisy, Third World city. Or they may have been cut off from the outside world for months at a time. They have changed, but they may not realize it until they transition "home" for retirement. Their values grow much less materialistic than those held by secular individuals. Their values seem much more spiritually oriented than the average secular individual. The average minister lives and sacrifices for ministry. Most secular individuals fail to understand that value, preferring to pursue happiness.

In fundamental ways, the retiring minister seems very different than the average secular individual.

Second, consider that the home country and the people left behind have also changed. Another expatriate says, "Upon re-entry to the native culture without adequate preparation, people are likely to discover, much to their surprise, that they cannot simply pick up where they left off. Their friends, family members, and work associates did not go into hibernation while they were away." Frequently, "old friends" have slowly digressed into nothing more than acquaintances. Some died. All of them found new close friends, and the retirement age minister may feel like an "outsider" even among old childhood friends.

Third, consider that when ministers retire, the magnitude of the change deeply impacts their self-esteem. They not only change jobs, but they also change residences, sometimes speak another language, develop new daily habits, establish new social networks, adapt to a new culture, and modify their ministry roles. Thus, their entire identity seems to change.

The change in ministry seems difficult for some, particularly those who transition from a public speaking ministry to an isolated support ministry or a life of near-total retirement. To work through this reverse culture shock and self-esteem shock, ministers need to make their relationship with the Lord an even higher priority. If ministers build a meaningful relationship with God during the stresses and shocks of transitioning to another ministry, they can see God using them even through their fatigue and doubts. They will see God bringing people that help them gain a new perspective. More than anything, they will communicate to others that they don't have to be perfect to be used; that struggling with change is acceptable; and that God wants to use the average person in the average pew in the average church to fulfill His plan for the world.

Structure and schedule act as an antidote for chaos. Carefully plan and develop new structures and new schedules for each area of your life.

Reflection:

Now that you are "entering retirement," what experience or change in your own attitude has most affected how you relate to others?

When you are sharing with someone who changes the subject in the middle of the conversation or acts disinterested, how will you probably react to this, emotionally?

What changes during your absence from your "home" culture are noteworthy?

Evaluate the way you would communicate "right now" if you were to express honestly your heart attitude and feelings. Which of the following would best characterize the spirit of your communication? (Please note that these are all normal feelings during retirement transition.)

_____Pressure builds up inside me to the point of explosion.

_____I trust the Lord to communicate through me.

_____I withdraw and stop communicating.

_____I don't have anything to offer to anyone here.

_____I speak kindly and gently.

_____I talk continually.

_____None of the above is applicable.

Worthlessness

Stokes (1992, 116) states, "Any crisis of identity is accentuated by the fact that occupational identity is a primary means by which society defines a person and they define themselves. Loss of the work role does not establish what the new identity of the retired person should be, and lack of a defined role may lead to feelings of worthlessness and low self-esteem." If Stokes is correct, no wonder that ministers (and especially missionaries and chaplains) facing retirement commonly report feelings of worthlessness.

Feelings of worthlessness result as the minister perceives that others view him or her as finished, without further value, or without much importance. Sometimes, their self-worth gets damaged by events on the field or at a recent church assignment or, more frequently, by the transition process itself. Because of the complexity of rebuilding self-esteem, chapter 7 addresses this topic more fully.

Ambiguity

Ambiguity is a sense that life includes little or no connectedness. One no longer feels as if he or she belongs to a team, has status, or has intimacy with any work group. Commonly, a missionary or chaplain will retain "sacred objects" such as photographs, souvenirs, and cultural objects to remember the time at which he or she felt connected to others. This is appropriate even though others may not understand one's desire to retain these objects. David Pollock frequently noted that those in transition possess "special knowledge without use"—knowledge that no one seems able to use. Accept their limitations. Their disinterest isn't due to a disinterest in you, but a background that lacks any knowledge about your experiences and culture.

Anxiety

Anxiety induces feelings of emotional instability, sometimes accompanied by a feeling of losing one's mind or suffering from a nervous breakdown. Sometimes, one may experience nightmares such as dreams of death, loss of a loved one, or loss of a body part. Anxiety includes:

- A sense of isolation, of "What am I doing here? Will I ever adjust?" "No one understands me."
- A sense of self-centeredness resulting from frustration.

Grief

Any job change, especially retirement for a minister, can stimulate intense grief. The minister grieves not only about losing a job assignment and close relationships, but about the potential of losing his or her God-given identity as a minister.

The five "stages" of grief describe changes commonly experienced during the retirement process. The stages usually follow a predefined sequence but sometimes occur in random order. One may spend more time in one stage or even return to a stage several times before reaching acceptance. The five stages are commonly defined as:

Denial: Involves shock, disbelief, and protest. ("This can't be happening to me! There must be some mistake.")

Anger: Involves feeling irritable, withdrawn, often demanding, questioning God. ("Why me? This is not fair!")

Bargaining: Includes a response between anger and depression during which the individual may make promises or resolutions, or issue ultimatums and threats in an attempt to regain control of circumstances and thus get a grip on reality.

Depression: Characterized by hopelessness, guilt, extreme sadness, indifference, low energy, loss of libido, sleep disturbance, and loss of appetite.

Acceptance: Because grief is a normal human process, there is no "cure." However, you can gradually learn to accept it.

Developing Sections 4 and 5 of Your Retirement Plan

C. L. Hastons, a retired missionary who subsequently re-entered full-time missionary work, when asked what he would tell ministers getting ready to retire, said, "Plan on it. Plan purposefully and completely. Don't retire without detailed plans." This truth applies to anyone retiring, ministers alike. Ernie Zelinski, in *How to Retire Happy, Wild, and Free* notes: "To not plan for an active retirement is to set yourself up for a difficult one" (2005, 14).

Consider for a moment—pastors without goals usually feel devastated when their church suddenly asks them to leave or retire. Without meaningful goals across all domains of life, their hope and self-worth are easily obliterated when their ministry goals get suddenly blocked. Can you identify how retirement could affect you, similarly? How will you feel if you suddenly find that no ministry exists for you in the future? Sir Francis Bacon, said, "A wise man will make more opportunities than he finds." Indeed, a wise minister will also make goals across more domains in life than ministry, alone.

The chapter on leaving covered the first three domains, a plan for work/ministry, a plan for financial security, and a plan for academic growth. Regardless, a minister's plan for ministry often gets firmly blocked during the initial steps of retirement transition and re-entry. That is, no matter how well a minister plans the transition into a new or different ministry, unseen events can block the best-laid plans temporarily. When our goals conflict with each other or get firmly blocked, physical illness and depression often result (Emmons, 1999, 75). This aspect of goal development affects well-being more than any other characteristic about goals (Ibid., 60). Thus, limiting retirement goals to the first three domains covered in the previous chapter leaves a minister susceptible to burnout and depression. C. R. Snyder, in the *Handbook of Hope* (1994, 147) describes the broad goal domains that stimulate hopeful thinking. The Transition Stage provides opportunity to develop goals in two more of these domains.

Retirement Plan Section 4: Spiritual Intimacy

The transition stage seems characterized by chaos. The best antidote to chaos comes from pursuing spiritual intimacy with the Lord. As we sit in the presence of the Prince of Peace, inner chaos cannot persist.

What are your goals for spiritual intimacy during retirement? Note that these are not ministry goals; these are goals to deepen your personal relationship with God. Emmons (1999, 108) notes that spiritual strivings provide an "empowering function" that "can confer coherence upon the personality." That is, spiritual strivings integrate all of one's other strivings "in the face of constant environmental and cultural pressures that push for fragmentation." Thus, spiritual strivings, more than any other strivings, act to integrate and stabilize the minister going through retirement transition. "The hallmark of the psychologically healthy person is integration" (Ibid., 118).

David Augsburger (2006, 96) quotes from Koontz (1996, 83-84) the words of Dr. Erland Waltner, who wrote, at the age of eighty:

> During the last decade of my life…I have sensed I am in transition on my experience of God…. For many years my

time with God was something like a quick stop while driving on a long and sometimes rough road...a pit stop in the Indianapolis 500 when drivers stop to refuel, to check tires, to watch for possible troubles ahead before hurrying back to the fast lane as quickly as possible. I called mine a "spirituality of the road."

Now I am beginning to see my relationship with God as being like a river which helps me get from here to there, to carry me almost from day to day, from task to task, from one experience to the next. I am experiencing God as One who is not only daily present with me but One [who] is in motion, bearing me up, sustaining, renewing, and enabling me.

Spirituality of the river asks for a higher kind of trusting in God, a deeper kind of love, a profound hope to be carried on by this river.

- What account do you hope to give for your spiritual life?

- Is the life that you lived the one that you wanted to live?

- What can you afford to do with your life, now?

- At what time of the day will you maintain daily devotions?

- How long will you spend daily in prayer?

- How long will you spend daily in Bible study? How long will you journal the insights that God provides?

- With whom, and how will you connect to reflect about what God is revealing to you?

Should I Journal?

William Bridges, in his book *Transitions: Making Sense of Life's Changes* (1980) offers this as his first suggestion for how to find meaning during this stage. Many retirees find journaling as one of the most important activities in retirement. Begin a spiritual journal of your experiences: (What is really going on? What are my mood and thoughts at the time? What unusual things are happening? What decisions can I make? What dreams am I having?). Initiate writing your autobiography or a daily journal. In all activities, however, find where God remains present. Some ministers describe the transition stage as a time when they feel as if they are treated like an appliance that can be unplugged and plugged back in again at will. Please spend a few days alone to reflect consciously on your feelings during retirement transition. When you compare your feelings to Bridge's suggestions above, how do you feel?

Find Ways to Appreciate the Past and the Present

Emmons (1999, 172) reports a study he conducted with Crumpler in which they examined gratitude. One-third of the subjects were asked simply to record five events that affected them during the past week, one-third were asked to record five hassles that affected them during the past week, and one-third were asked to record five things during the past week for which they were grateful. Relative to the other groups, the grateful group felt better about their lives, were more optimistic about the upcoming week, spent significantly more time exercising, and reported having made more progress toward their goals. The study provides evidence that "thanksgiving leads to having more to give thanks for," and that "counting one's blessings, one by one" produces "successful life functioning" (173).

Psychologist Mitchel Adler (2001) defines the following eight aspects of appreciation. Each time you go through the transition stage, thoroughly evaluate your appreciation in each of these aspects.

Possession focus—what do you have for which you are appreciative? (Note that what you have is not confined to material possessions, but also includes intangible possessions.)

- What are your blessings in this world, both now and after retirement?
- What privileges are you bringing with you, now, as you transition into retirement?
- What are your opportunities even as you face retirement?
- For what are you fortunate?
- What are the good things you have in life, after retirement?

Awe—what makes you sometimes stand in awe?

- How has God been involved in your life and ministry?
- What past events lead you to realize that you are really fortunate to be alive?
- What, in nature, helps you feel emotionally connected to God?
- What miracles is God still performing in your life and in the lives of those you love?

Rituals—what specific acts or rituals do you use to give thanks to the Lord and to others?

- What specific rituals or events remind you to give thanks on a regular basis?

- How often do you remind yourself purposefully to give thanks?

Present moment—in what ways do you stop to appreciate the present moment even while you are experiencing it? e.g.:
- Nature
- Work and ministry
- Other individuals
- Other events

Social comparison—by remembering some individuals who are less fortunate than yourself, are you periodically reminded to take note of how fortunate you are, especially in retirement?

Gratitude—for what do you have gratitude?
- List the sacrifices others have made on your behalf for which you are presently grateful.
- Do you feel gratitude for emotional or monetary debts that you can never repay? List those debts.
- What are some of the opportunities you have experienced for which you feel grateful?
- For what are you especially thankful to God (what has He done uniquely for you)?

Loss and adversity—what personal losses and adversities have reminded you of how fortunate you really are?
- What personal problems and challenges in life remind you to value the positive aspects of life?
- What, in particular, reminds you to live every day to the fullest?

Interpersonal relationships—for what interpersonal relationships are you appreciative?

- Who really cares about you?
- Who understands you?

Retirement Plan Section 5: Personal Intimacy

Just like spiritual intimacy grounds a minister during the chaos of transition, so personal intimacy with your spouse or closest friend also provides support from chaos. What are your goals for intimacy with your spouse or closest friend? To whom will you talk about your deepest troubles and feelings? Please note that for singles, intimacy includes the friendship of a closest friend. Unmarried ministers often overlook their need for intimacy, even with close friends. How will you develop and maintain intimacy, and with whom?

- How often will you talk?
  - Daily schedule—
  - Weekly schedule—
- Where will you talk?

- What else will you do to foster deeper intimacy?

CHAPTER 5

The
Entering
Stage

Not that I have already attained all this, or have already been made perfect, but I press on to take hold of that for which Christ Jesus took hold of me. Brothers, I do not consider myself to have yet taken hold of it. But one thing I do: forgetting what is behind and straining for what is ahead, I press on toward the goal to win the prize for which God has called me heavenward in Christ Jesus. Philippians 3: 12-14 (NIV)

The entering stage includes those who have started working in their new retirement ministry and implementing their new retirement lifestyle. Superficiality, an introduction to newness, and vulnerability characterize the entering stage. Inevitably, the harder a minister works at developing and implementing the *entering* section of their retirement plan, the more satisfying their retirement.

Superficiality

You may feel that you are treated superficially during the entering stage. After all, others probably do not know you as deeply as those in your previous ministry. Since they don't know you deeply, they may treat you superficially based on characteristics such as your dress, temperament, housing, and immediately observable accomplishments. Many ministers feel emotionally devastated whenever someone questions their commitment and integrity. However, without any prior history of your commitment and integrity, they may question you regularly. This is normal. Conversely, you may find yourself questioning the commitment and integrity of your new local pastor. Without historical precedent, we tend to treat others superficially, especially those from a North American culture. And, many other cultures also value a superficial money-based, power-based, and status-based orientation.

The entering stage is a time for observing new cultural values in your local church and the culture in your local town. The more you discuss, reflect and journal these differences, the better you adjust. Approach the entering stage as you might approach an assignment to an entirely new ministry in a new country. Gather information and discuss your insights with others.

If you returning to the USA, you are entering a culture that probably seems extremely individualistic compared to others; and, your retirement location may seem even more individualistic than the culture in which you worked as a minister. In your new church, therefore, others may value you more for the superficiality of your productivity than for your character, your prior history, or your prior status. Others may act more interested in promoting their individual differences and personal recognition than in maintaining harmony in your local church. Others may seem more interested in discovering their own pathway to spiritual growth than in asking for wisdom from a seasoned minister like you. For ministers entering retirement, the individualistic Westernized cultures may seem very superficial.

You may find large cultural differences in values about identity, communication styles, responsibility, control, uncertainty, time, and power. Please note that you will need to adapt to them—they remain unable to adapt to you. Adaptation never means that you accept their values but that you remain determined to work with them in spite of their values.

The majority of North Americans value principles over relationships, that is, they value their principles above your relationship. Your relationship with friends and family may not survive unless you willing discuss all aspects of every principle and work with individuals who devalue your personal principles.

The majority of North Americans separate the person from the person's words or actions, that is, they rarely care if your family position or church leadership position gives you the right to talk—they firmly value their insights as much or more than yours. You may need to discuss and defend issues as if other church members are peers even when they know little about the issue being discussed.

The North American culture remains unique in the world, and possibly very different from the culture in which you last worked. Most importantly, the North American culture actively devalues retired individuals. During the entering stage, observe, ask nonjudgmental questions, learn, and seek understanding.

North Americans tend to employ rationalizations and relativistic values—while they believe that it is okay to challenge values, a judgmental attitude and absolute values remain unacceptable to them. The individuals in your retirement culture may not understand or respond to the indirect confrontational strategies that you so carefully learned elsewhere.

Introduction to Newness

Take time to find a good mentor (or mentors) to assist you during the entering stage. *Don't leave this to chance!* Note that a good mentor often views issues differently than you do, but he or she will help you explore all aspects of your retirement plan. Develop a specific plan to review your monthly progress toward each part of your retirement plan with one or more mentors. Contact the mentors and set up a recurring meeting, e.g., 10:00 a.m. the second Tuesday morning of each month. Thoroughly discuss the values and cultural differences that you find annoying. Allow that person to act as your "cultural informant" or bridge-builder toward retirement.

Avoid latching onto the first mentor available. Those mentors most available usually remain available for a good reason—no one else wants them as a mentor. Some individuals want to mentor others out of their own need for control, recognition, status, or acceptance. Select a retirement mentor who is retired, still engaged in ministry, and energetically pursuing each of the ten goal domains discussed in this book. Probe how that individual pursues each of the goal domains. A healthy mentor can easily relate his or her retirement transition experience to several goal areas. However, you may need several mentors, each experienced with different types of goals.

Vulnerability

Many individuals feel vulnerable during the entering stage. Due to vulnerability, behaviors may become exaggerated. For instance, one may easily conclude, "I'll never get used to driving as fast as they do in this city. I'll always feel abnormal. I'll never get back to me. I'll always feel off-balance." However, any statement that starts with a "never" statement is almost never correct, and any statement that starts with an "always" statement is almost always wrong. You *will* adjust to the new culture and to retirement, but it almost always takes time and hard work. North America remains a difficult country for retirement adjustment—the culture devalues retired individuals.

One may easily conclude that he or she may avoid vulnerability if employed by a local church. However, few occupations remain more vulnerable than working in a local church. For all of the superficial reasons stated above, few retired ministers find security in a local church position. Of course, ministers who reach retirement age rarely value security, or they would never have responded to a call into ministry. Retired ministers offer a plethora of skills to any local church. When offered with humility, the retired minister can mentor new Christians in any culture, including North America.

Sometimes, the individual in transition feels tempted to break God's rules or his or her own rules. For instance, some ministers dutifully engage in daily devotions prior to retirement but fail to follow through during retirement transition.

You will feel vulnerable. The apostles expressed vulnerability, and even Jesus, himself, expressed vulnerability. Madeleine L. Engle stated, "When we were children, we used to think that when we were grown-up we would no longer be vulnerable. But to grow up is to accept vulnerability... To be alive is to be vulnerable." Ministry is not about obtaining financial security or avoiding risk. Ministry is not about finding happiness or avoiding vulnerability. It is strictly a matter of obedience and relationship with God. Retirement provides a time of vulnerability— so what? We can trust God, even in the midst of our vulnerability, to remain with us.

Retirement Plan Section 6:
Family Goals

What specific new family goals seem meaningful to pursue during retirement? A physical separation from their relatives blocks many ministers from pursuing family oriented goals. For retirement, you may want to develop specific goals toward your family, either to develop closer relationships or to help guide the next generation. Consider your potentially changing role toward family members, e.g., you may change from active work to advising and mentoring. Consider any need to help aging parents, ailing spouses, or needy grandchildren. Consider if you need to move physically closer to your family to accomplish your family goals. How can you balance your need to remain independent (not enmeshed) in the lives of parents and children who cannot care for themselves, even while offering care to those same individuals?

- What are my goals for strengthening my family relationships?

    - My children–

    - My brothers/sisters–

    - My parents –

    - Others –

- What are the first three steps toward these goals?

- What might slow me down or stop me from making my family goals?

- What are some alternative pathways to reach my goal?

Retirement Plan Section 7: Health and Fitness

For ministers of retirement age, some of the most important daily schedules include those that enable the pursuit of physical health and prevent the illness and disability common to those in retirement. Most individuals try to recreate structure from a previous period of life. Although this may seem appropriate for other life-stage transitions, middle-age habits often include behaviors unhealthy for retirement. Recreating middle-age structure often leads to premature death for a retiree. Many diseases and disabilities previously thought inherent for retirement can be prevented, or at the least, slowed for decades. Preventable diseases related to aging include cancer, heart disease, stroke, osteoporosis, dementia, and depression. Although cancer, heart disease, and stroke may occur in middle-aged ministers prior to retirement, the post-retirement risk soars much higher. Unlike other life transitions, *successful* retirement almost always requires an entirely new lifestyle, one that avoids the risk factors common to a middle-age lifestyle. To learn more about the medical issues discussed below, please talk to your physician.

What are your goals for pursuing health and fitness during retirement? Physical activity increases one's positive outlook and helps to keep one mentally sharp (Hill, Storandt, & Malley, 1993). Fortunately, physical fitness usually results from a simple choice. Daily aerobic exercise and weight training ranks as one of the most important retirement lifestyle choices. Brisk walking, as simple as it seems, offers one of the easiest routes to aerobic fitness. Weight training not only increases strength, but it also stimulates weight loss, reduces depression, and strengthens bones. However you do it, choose to exercise one hour per day, five days per week. Find a specific time to schedule exercise into your daily pattern. If you fail to schedule a specific time for exercise, it probably will not happen.

Retirees often assume that their previous middle-age diet and exercise regimen worked satisfactorily, and therefore remains adequate for the retiree. Nothing could be further from the truth. The risk factors associated with poor diet and lack of exercise soar about ten times higher after age 65 than during the middle age years. In short, you may survive a lifestyle characterized by poor nutrition and lack of exercise during middle age, but almost no one survives that lifestyle for very long after retirement. For instance, very few obese men survive to 80-years of age with a body mass index above 30, and none survive past 80-years of age with a body mass index above 35. Retaining a sedentary middle-age diet and exercise regimen almost guarantees physical problems associated with obesity, hypertension, heart disease, stroke, osteoporosis, and dementia. For most ministers, retiring *successfully* means adopting an entirely new lifestyle that promotes entirely new behaviors. It is NOT a matter of implementing the new lifestyle for a short period of time to get in shape; instead, it is a matter of promoting these new behaviors for a lifetime.

A few ministers accept outdated beliefs that undermine health and fitness. One minister said, "One day less on earth due to premature death simply provides one more day with the Lord." Such a belief fails to recognize the value of life, the joy of ministering for the Lord for as long as possible, and the joy of mentoring other humans in their spiritual walk. It fails to acknowledge truthfully that another day with the Lord seems almost meaningless when compared to eternity, while another day serving Him in ministry provides eternal benefits to others. God calls ministers to serve, not to die prematurely.

A minister friend said, "I might as well burn out in a frenzy of work because the Lord will return before I die." The Lord may return during our lifetime, but no one can predict the time of the Lord's return, including whether it will occur during our lifetime or 100 generations later. Meanwhile, a few individuals squander the potential of long-term retirement ministry to justify a short-term frenzy of overwork and poor health management, all while trying to fortune-tell what remains unpredictable.

Obedience to the call of ministry includes the choice to prolong health and service as much as possible. My plan for health and fitness includes:

- Good sleep patterns of:
    - I will start getting ready for bed at…
    - I will go to bed at…
    - I will rise at…
    - I will …
    - I will …
- Eat a healthy, balanced diet:
    - I will avoid foods such as …

    - I will try to increase my intake of foods such as…

- I will try to maintain a body weight of …

- Exercise daily (M-F)—45 minutes to 1 hour of ...
  - o   I will obtain exercise through the following activities

  - o   I will exercise at the following time of the day ...

  - o   I will try to obtain exercise accountability by enlisting the following individuals to exercise with me ...

  - o   My weekly exercise schedule will be as follows:

  - o   I will pursue other physical activity (e.g., biking, swimming, and hiking) 1-2 times a month:

- Medication—I will take the following medication and supplements:

Preventing cancer. Cancer prevention is generally based on early detection and prevention. For many cancers, the most proven measure of prevention requires early detection by physical exam, PAP smears, a colonoscopy, and PSA testing. Other than early detection, carefully follow your physician's recommendations, especially about preventing breast cancer.

Preventing heart disease. A high level of HDL cholesterol provides a protective effect against heart disease. HDL cholesterol is commonly called the "good cholesterol." Exercise and/or medication provide potential interventions for those with a low HDL level.

Hypertension, commonly called "high-blood pressure" provides a second primary risk factor. Talk to your physician about hypertension and especially about Isolated Systolic Hypertension (indicated when the upper blood pressure number is above 140mmHg). Inexpensive diuretics usually provide an effective treatment for hypertension. Daily exercise, medication, and a low salt diet seem to prevent hypertension. Syndrome X constitutes a third primary risk factor. Syndrome X represents a family of risky behaviors including obesity, a tendency toward diabetes, high blood pressure, and high blood fats. However, diet and exercise almost totally prevent Syndrome X. Thus, simple changes in diet, exercise, and the use of relatively low-cost diuretics prevent all of the above primary risk factors.

Preventing stroke. Prevent stroke by preventing high blood pressure. Also consult your physician about the best way to prevent a stroke based on your family history.

Preventing osteoporosis. Osteoporosis is a common risk factor as one ages, especially common among thin and small-boned Caucasian women. However, osteoporosis also occurs with other females and males as they age. As bones become increasingly thinner, they eventually break. When this happens in the spinal column, serious complications can result. During a fall, when a hip fractures, the individual often tries to break the fall with his or her hand, causing a wrist fracture. Thus, multiple fractures can result. In addition to early detection through screening, prevention measures include hormone replacement therapy for females, calcium dietary supplements, and daily exercise. Ask your doctor about taking a daily calcium supplement.

For most individuals, exercise seems preferable to medication, and should almost always be implemented even with medication. Weight lifting exercise seems to help prevent bone loss, and also increases bone density.

Preventing dementia. Many factors cause dementia, but the more common forms of dementia include multi-infarct dementia and Alzheimer's disease. Any lifestyle that prevents hypertension (such as daily exercise, a strict low-sodium and low-saturated-fat diet) helps prevent multi-infarct dementia. Always ask your doctor about implementing prevention measures to reduce complications specific to you. If you have any question about early dementia, please ask your doctor about getting a memory or brain function test.

Using vaccination to prevent disease. The annual influenza vaccination protects aging adults against a very serious threat. Influenza remains extremely dangerous and life-threatening to adults over 60 years of age. Prevent influenza with simple yearly vaccination. Many doctors and communities offer a free vaccination for those over sixty years of age. Pneumonia is also common and often fatal to older adults. A single vaccination offers long-term protection. If you received the vaccination before age sixty-five, talk to your doctor to see if another vaccination is needed. A tetanus vaccination also protects against a common and often fatal disease for those over age sixty. Consider getting a booster vaccination every ten years. Also, ask your doctor about getting a vaccination for shingles.

Preventing depression. Depression is much more common among retirees than among the general population. Many factors cause depression, but Dr. Steve Ilardi, a psychologist with the University of Kansas, found six specific lifestyles that seem to prevent depression. However, these six lifestyles seem increasingly difficult in modern society. Over the past thirty years, the depression rate has increased ten-fold. Dr. Steve Ilardi notes that the six lifestyles not only help prevent depression, but these same lifestyles also help stimulate recovery from depression (Ilardi, Karwoski, Lehman, Stites, and Steidtmann, 2007):

1. *Omega-3.* Mounting evidence points to a strong link between the decrease in omega-3 fatty acid consumption and increased rates of depression (Hibbeln and Salem, 1999). Although the modern North American diet now has a 16:1 ratio of omega-6 to omega-3 fatty acids, a 1:1 ratio seems to help prevent depression (Nemets, Stahl, & Belmaker, 2002; Peet & Horrobin, 2002; Nemets et. al., 2006). Generally, a 1000 mg daily omega-3 supplement returns the ratio close to 1:1. At the time of this writing, an economical source is Omega-3 Mood Formula by Vitacost. Dr. Ilardi notes the need for omega-3 fatty acids:

     Dietary omega-3 fatty acids are key building blocks of brain tissue that can only be obtained from diet (the body can't make them), and dietary omega-3 deficiency is an enormously important risk factor for depression. Most Americans are deficient, but those who are depressed have much lower blood/brain levels than the rest of us. By far the most effective way of ensuring adequate intake is to use a good fish oil supplement to obtain a daily dose of 1000mg of the omega-3 molecule called EPA. It should also be a molecularly distilled supplement to ensure minimal exposure to mercury/heavy metal toxins that are potentially present in fish oil.

2. *Sunlight.* Many ministers spend most of their daylight hours indoors either at school or in an office environment. Direct sunlight provides about 10,000 foot lamberts—generally 50-100 times brighter than indoor light. Exposure to at least thirty minutes of bright sunlight every day stimulates the brain to produce brain-healthy chemicals. Even when outdoors, many individuals fail to obtain enough direct sunlight due to their

climate or due to significant air pollution. Kuller (2002), Rosenthal (1993), Kripke (1998), and Tuunainen, Kripke, & Enco (2004) find that exposure to as little as 30 minutes of light from a 10,000 lux light-box protects against depression. These light-boxes may be purchased through the Internet for as little as $160. Some individuals bound to desk jobs use the light-box as an area light next to their computer.

3. *Sleep.* Humankind was designed to sleep at night. However, modern society provides artificial light that enables us to stay up until 10 or 11 PM each night. The average North American sleeps only 6.8 hours nightly (National Sleep Foundation, 2005). Morawetz (2003) found evidence that 8-9 hours of sleep is needed to protect against depression. Eugene Peterson (1987, 66-74) notes that the biblical Sabbath begins daily at sundown, not at sunrise. Eugene Peterson notes that Sabbath occurs every day. Thus, each day begins with a Sabbath rest at sundown, and then concludes as "we wake and are called out to participate in God's creative action (Ibid., 68)." When we neglect to start each day with adequate rest, we violate one of the Ten Commandments and inhibit our ability to fully participate in God's creative action. Arguably, God's Sabbath commandment provides as much physical health as spiritual health.

4. *Aerobic exercise.* Prehistoric man experienced 2-3 hours of daily exercise, often traveling up to 10 miles per day (Cordain, Gotshall, Eaton & Eaton, 1998). Over the past 50 years, North Americans increasingly work at sedentary jobs. Stephens (1988), and Ross and Hayes (1988) found evidence that 30 minutes of aerobic exercise helps to prevent depression by influencing the amount of serotonin produced

within the brain. As little as 30 minutes of daily aerobic exercise has been found to be as effective as Zoloft in treating depression, and with a lower relapse rate (Blumenthal et al., 1999, 2001).

5. *Interdependent social interaction.* Some individuals find deep interpersonal relationships difficult due to physical and cultural isolation. Expatriates, upon re-entry back to the States, sometimes retain the same meager social relationship style that they used overseas. However, deep interpersonal relationships help to prevent depression (Elkin et al, 1989; de Mello, de Jesus, Bacaltchuk, Verdeli & Neugebauer, 2005). Dr. Ilardi notes, "We're hard-wired to crave social support in the form of visual interaction each day with people who care about us; i.e., we need face time with friends and loved ones."

6. *Anti-ruminative activities.* When individuals ruminate about a negative thought or event, they grow susceptible to depression (Just & Alloy, 1997; Nolen-Hoeksema, 1991). Even the common act of watching television promotes rumination (Cropley & Purvis, 2003). Since the average North American spends about 30 hours per week watching television, the average North American may easily spend more time engaging in ruminative thoughts than individuals from countries in which television remains unavailable. Those who employ alternative consuming activities, such as getting totally absorbed in a hobby or physical sport, tend to prevent depression (Dimidjian et al, 2006; Wells & Papageorgiou, 2003). Whenever one finds himself or herself engaging in negative rumination, they can replace those thoughts with an alternative totally engaging activity, such as a hobby or a

sport. Meditative prayer provides the most effective protection against negative rumination. In this form of prayer, the individual ceases to bring his or her personal problems (ruminative thoughts and "to do" lists) to God, but simply spends focused time worshipping and being with God. One cannot ruminate on personal problems when he or she focuses fully on the creator. The "thankfulness" exercise in this book also reduces negative rumination.

Federal Government Websites Providing Health-Care Related Information

Healthfinder provides a gateway site to help consumers find health and human services information quickly. Healthfinder includes links to more than 1,250 Web sites, including more than 250 federal sites and 1,000 state, local, not-for-profit, university and other consumer health resources.

MEDLINEplus is a service of the National Library of Medicine, provides a rich array of evaluated health and disease-related web resources for the consumer.

National Institute on Aging promotes healthy aging by conducting and supporting biomedical, social, behavioral research, and public education.

NIH Health Information Page provides a single access point to the consumer health information resources of the National Institutes of Health, including the NIH Health Information Index, NIH publications and clearinghouses and the Combined Health Information Database.

PubMed is a service of the National Library of Medicine, provides access to over 11 million MEDLINE citations back to the mid-1960's and additional life science journals. PubMed includes links to many sites providing full text articles and other related resources.

MEDLINE is the world's most extensive collection of published medical information, coordinated by the National Library of Medicine.

Veterans Benefits—The U.S. Department of Veterans Affairs administers many programs for veterans. See their Web site for information about benefits, facilities, programs for senior veterans, the facts about enrollment for VA health care and more. Check out their 1-Stop Service Inquiry Page.

Partners for Prescription Assistance is a prescription assistance program that brings together America's pharmaceutical companies, doctors, patient advocacy organizations and civic groups to help low-income, uninsured patients get free or nearly free brand-name medicines.

Rx Outreach is a new Patient Assistance Program developed by Express Scripts Specialty Distribution Services, Inc. (ESSDS). The program provides qualified low-income individuals and families with access to generic versions of brand name medications.

U-Share is a prescription drug discount card. The U Share Prescription Drug Discount Card provides discounts on all Medicare-allowed prescription drugs.

Needymeds is a patient assistance program that provides no-cost prescription medications to eligible participants.

CHAPTER 6

 The Re-Involvement Stage

The ordinary man is involved in action, the hero acts. An immense difference. —Henry Miller

The re-involvement stage occurs as the retiree re-engages fully in a new ministry role, and feels adjusted to a new retirement lifestyle. The retiree feels a renewed sense of status in which people once again know him or her, and know his or her roles. And, at an emotional level, the retiree feels loved, valued and appreciated. At last, he or she re-engages with their entirely new lifestyle. The re-involvement stage usually lasts at least two years. If the retiree suffers from a progressive disease, he or she may barely reach the re-involvement stage before needing to start the transition process all over again.

Key Aspects of Re-Involvement

Situation

During re-involvement, the retiree usually wants to reflect on his or her roles, and position on a ministry team, social network, and family clan. During the re-involvement stage, reassess the status across all the goal domains developed in your retirement plan. After referencing the goals in your retirement plan, continue to refine them with the following considerations:

- What is my new position/role within my ministry team, within my social network, and within my extended family? Is this role what I expected, and am I comfortable with it?

- How well am I progressing toward achieving each goal in my retirement plan? Is my progress toward each goal appropriate for the re-involvement stage? What do I need to change to improve progress toward each of my retirement goals?

- Am I really thriving at meaningful ministry? What do I need to do to thrive more?

- Have I been able to maintain a productive ministry in spite of mundane daily tasks such as helping aging parents, helping ailing spouses, helping needy grandchildren, and setting up a new house?

- Have I been able to maintain a productive ministry in spite of the North American culture that influences me to retire to a lifestyle of self-indulgence and leisure? How well am I balancing my freedom in retirement with responsibility to God?

- Is my ministry at risk due to any outside influences (debt, law-suits, conflict, organizational change, etc.)? How can I control those influences, or do I need to adjust or modify my ministry, due to one or more of these influences?

- Is my ministry at risk due to any chronic influences such as a progressive illness? Do I need to adjust or modify my ministry due to a progressive illness or other chronic influence?

- Am I under too much stress? What is causing the stress— family, environment, my goals, crises, conflicts? With whom can I talk about those stressors?

Self

Assess if you are known and accepted not only for the work that you accomplish, but also for your unique personality characteristics and personal lifestyle behaviors. What new strengths and weaknesses have you found during the retirement transition process (work skills, personality traits, socialization skills, emotional state)? Consider:

- How well am I doing at pursuing physical health?

- Do I really believe and behave as if I have alternative pathways?

- Am I behaving optimistically, or do I have difficulty dealing with ambiguity? If I am not optimistic about my retirement, who can continually help me to discover the positive aspects of my transition?

- What are some ways that I can still better develop myself during retirement (education, mentoring, short courses, career counseling, relationship counseling)?

- How am I doing emotionally? If you are experiencing depression or burnout symptoms, please see a medical doctor immediately. Often, it is difficult to notice these symptoms in yourself. Whom can I ask (a spouse or close friend) to monitor me? How will I reduce stress when I feel totally stressed out?

- How will I cultivate a strong hedge—highly secure, well-guarded spiritual and emotional boundaries that I will protect even during my retirement transition? Unless one intentionally cultivates strong boundaries, the boundaries are easily violated during retirement. How will I cultivate strong and secure attachments with others even while building a strong hedge against moral infidelity? How will I develop openness with others?

- Am I using retirement to withdraw, or to remain active and alert?

- Am I still drawing ever closer to God during retirement?

Strategies

Please reference your retirement plan. The pathways toward your retirement goals outline your strategies for re-involvement. During the re-involvement stage, reassess and refine these pathways. Consider:

- How much are your mentors helping you? Do you need to develop additional mentors?

- Can you host a "re-involvement review" with all your mentors to review your plans, your progress along the pathways, and to brainstorm refinements to your strategies?

- If you foresee that you will eventually become too disabled to host a "re-involvement review," can you put together a team of close friends and loved ones who will annually re-assess and brainstorm ideas about your situation, self, strategies, and supports?

Supports

Social support by far remains the most important factor affecting the well-being of the ministerial retiree. Rowe and Kahn, in *Successful Aging*, state, "Being part of a social network of friends and family is one of the most dependable predictors of longevity" (1999, 46). "The more that older people participate in social relationships, the better their overall health" (Ibid., 163). They define social support as: "information leading one to believe that he or she is cared for, loved, esteemed and a member of a network of mutual obligations" (Ibid., 157). Interactions between people who communicate such information protect them from many of the damaging health effects of stressful life events. Cohen, McGowan, Fooskas, and Rose (1984) found that perceived social support provides direct and stress-buffering protection.

To self-assess your social support structure, consider the following:

- Am I actively looking for emotional support?

- Am I acting apathetic?

- Am I sabotaging the process of developing supports? (Please note that apathy can sabotage the transition process as much as anything else.)

Buss (2000) recommends the following strategies to promote deeper social connectedness:

- Promote the aspect of your reputation that highlights your unique or exceptional attributes.

- Recognize your personal attributes that others tend to value but have difficulty getting from other people.

- Acquire specialized skills that make you irreplaceable.

- Seek out groups that most strongly value what you have to offer, and what others in the group tend to lack.

- Avoid groups where your unique attributes are not valued.

- Connect intentionally with individuals who have come to your aid during your times of crisis.

Retirement Plan Section 8: Friendships

Many ministers (especially missionaries and chaplains) retire with few close stateside friendships due to the distance and separation of their previous ministry. They maintain a multitude of casual pastoral friendships, but few intimate friendships at the location in which they choose to retire.

Many retired ministers find they feel emotionally closer to their missionary, chaplain, or other peers than to their parishioners, relatives, or neighbors. Consider whether you need to move physically closer to other retired ministers. Most ministers who retire to ministerial retirement communities highly recommend such a lifestyle due to the long-lasting relationships that come with that community.

What is your plan for developing and nurturing deep, meaningful relationships? Do you possess deep friendships that provide emotional support? Most ministers assume that their friendships remain much deeper than reality. Remember how little time you have spent in any single location. Johnson (217) lists the following characteristics of a supportive relationship:

- Objectivity and open-mindedness. You let others describe who they are and how they feel. You validate them.

- You support and affirm their individuality and recognize their strengths. You validate and encourage their goals.

- You empathize with them. You understand their life circumstances and how they are affected by their life experiences.

- You accept them as they are without being judgmental. You can ask one another for help and support.

- You can laugh with them and be playful. You will both enjoy it.

- You are at their side, supporting them to do whatever is important to them.

Try mapping your relationships to assess the strength of your support network. Identify the initials of each individual involved in your life and place him or her in one of the three circles on the relationship map below.

Those (other than your spouse and children) to whom you feel so close that it is hard to imagine life without them

Those who are important to you, and your relationship with them is close, but you know that you could adjust to life without

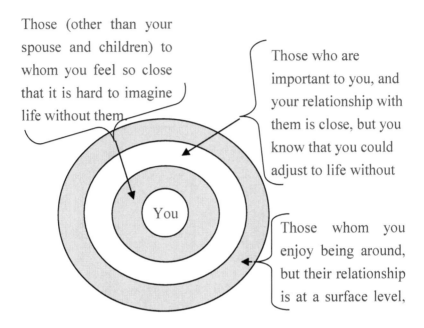

Those whom you enjoy being around, but their relationship is at a surface level,

Many ministers in retirement transition discover that they retain few or no peers (other than spouse and children) whom they would list in their inner circle. Each retiree should intentionally develop at least three individuals who fit within their inner circle.

Most retirees tend to develop friendships only with those who seem similar to them (about 5% of the population) and avoid others. If the retirement age minister enters retirement with this value, he or she will suffer from restricted resources for friendships. If any of the following characterize you, then you may possess limited friendship resources:

- Am I retiring in a location or church in which few individuals understand my previous ministry or the culture of my previous residence?

- Are my friendships conditional—that is, based on others being similar to me?

- Are my friendships limited by my health limitations?

- Do I have a limited history of deep personal involvement?

The deepest friendships remain possible even with those who seem extremely different from us (95% of the population). The deepest friendships almost always require acceptance of personality differences quite different from ours. After all, how many individuals from your local church can you realistically expect to understand the stresses of a world-traveled missionary or widely experienced minster?

The deepest friendships are based on sharing and accepting the other individual's interests, not your own interests. After all, you probably experienced a much broader palate of food, cultures, travel, and world events than the average retirement age individual. Thus, they cannot share your interests—they may not even understand your interests. As you accept them and their interests, they will gradually learn to accept you. A good prescription for deep friendships is: don't worry about what others think about you, worry about what you think of others.

To develop retirement friendships, please consider the following suggestions:

- Identify potential friends. Make a list of those who look friendly at church, in your neighborhood, and other places that you frequent.

- Appear friendly, yourself. Greet others with a smile or warm hello, laugh when appropriate, offer appropriate touch (a gentle hug, hand on the arm), and engage others with questions that show an interest in them.

- Sanctify (set aside) weekly time to make good memories with those on your "potential friends" list. Suggest activities to share, and at the end of the activity, plan for a future get-together. Friendships usually develop most quickly when you invite others into your home. Few places feel as intimate as your personal home.

- Listen to them. Few individuals desire a friend who "rattles" on and on about himself or herself. Ask about their experiences, listen, and paraphrase (called "active" listening) their conversation back to them.

- Make a specific plan for friendship that includes reminiscing about their good and difficult times, validating their recent and past experiences, and communicating weekly, if not more often.

- When getting together with prospective friends, connect at their emotional level, encouraging them to describe who they are and how they feel. This type of connection means connecting emotionally (empathize) with them based on their emotions and their life events, not yours. The differences in between you lessen if you focus on their emotions and life events.

- Offer to help them when needed.

- Avoid an emotional connection based on a jointly held negative belief or negative experience. Negatives held in common rarely make a deep, lasting friendship. Instead, reminiscing on negative values and experiences held in common prevents development of a truly meaningful deep relationship. What are some common negative values or experiences that ministers discuss and form relationships around? These negative experiences and individuals rarely form deep friendships.

- Share your feelings—the good, the bad, and the ugly, and let them share all of theirs without seeming judgmental. Share your joys and pains grant acceptance of theirs.

- To develop a true friend, remember: "A friend is someone who is delighted to see you and does not have any immediate plans for your improvement" (author unknown). Avoid fostering plans to improve the other individual. Improvement remains God's job. Others seek ways to become like Him as they see the fruit of the Spirit working in you.

- Guard confidentiality—no friendship survives long without it. A true friend encourages the other individual beyond his or her weakness even while granting acceptance. A break of fellowship occurs only if the other individual is unwilling to work on his or her problem and the problem is a moral issue. A friend's confidentiality remains unbroken even when the friendship is broken.

- When you feel offended, respond assertively, but not aggressively. It is always appropriate to say, "When you said that, I felt hurt (or unappreciated, unvalued, unaccepted, uncared for, etc.)." However, it is rarely appropriate to verbally attack or criticize another.

- If you disagree with an issue, let them know why you disagree without criticizing or acting irritable. Disagree through discussion and dialog, without personal criticism, cynical remarks, or "put-downs."

- Reject inappropriate sexual comments or advances. If you don't like it when someone flirts with you, let them know that you feel uninterested. Leave relationships in which you feel sexual pressure.

Ministers often spend hundreds of hours planning the details of transition, only to throw their plan away when they encounter the first difficulty. Even the best laid transition plan requires a periodic update. Resist discarding your transition plan—simply keep modifying it. The plan provides you a sense of control during times of inevitable chaos. Rigidity in your plan will leave you frustrated and defeated. If you take your plan to God daily, He will inspire your steps.

- The three to five individuals with whom I will try to develop an inner circle friendship are:

- What are the first three steps toward my friendship goals?

- What might slow me down or stop me from making my goal?

- What are some alternative pathways to reach my goal?

Retirement Plan Section 9:
Leisure

What are your practical leisure goals for retirement? Many ministers pursue multiple ministerial responsibilities for decades to the exclusion of any leisure goals. What leisure activities would you like to pursue (e.g., gardening, photography, photo editing, reading, cooking, violin, listening to your favorite music)? How will you go about developing skills for those leisure activities?

- What are my leisure goals?

- What are the first three steps toward my goal?

- What might slow me down or stop me from making my leisure goals?

- What are some alternative pathways to reach my goal?

Retirement Plan Section 10: Personal Growth

What are your goals for personal growth (learning new skills or hobbies) during retirement? For these goals, consider what inherently interests you, outside of ministry.

- What are my personal growth goals?

- What are the first three steps toward my personal growth goals?

- What might slow me down or stop me from making my personal growth goal?

- What are some alternative pathways to reach my goal?

Personal Exercise

1. Suppose you could design a beautiful day without any constraints of time or money. Close your eyes and think of what the most beautiful day conceivable would be like for you (design the day fancifully without any limitations of time or money). Describe what that day might look like?

2. What fundamental qualities made your day truly beautiful?

-

-

-

-

-

3. Explain why you might, or might not, be successful in living your first "beautiful day."

4. Using the fundamental qualities you outlined above, design a second beautiful day that is within the realm of possibility for you to live, currently, considering your time and money. Describe what that day might look like?

5. Are all the qualities of your first beautiful day truly beautiful? What about your second?

6. What might you now change about your perception of a beautiful day?

-

-

-

-

7. What actions might you take to achieve a "beautiful day" on a more regular basis?

-

-

-

-

-

8. How well does your conception of a beautiful day fit with the goals and strivings that you are presently planning for your retirement transition?

9. How well does your conception of a beautiful day fit with the goals and strivings that you are presently experiencing prior to retirement transition?

CHAPTER 7

Retiring

With

Self-Esteem

There is a Divine and Infinite potential within every soul, an intimate access to the mind of God and the passion of the Universe.–K. Allen Kay

Self-esteem is a realistic, appreciative opinion of oneself, based on accuracy and honesty—Schiraldi (Building Self-Esteem, 1993, 17)

- It is positive and honest about strengths.
- It is appreciative about growth potentials.

Self-worth, self-competence, and self-acceptance contribute to defining an individual's self-esteem (Johnson, 1997, 217).

What Develops Self-Esteem?

Self-esteem results from seeing a reflection (a mirror image) of ourselves as we interact with other individuals. That is, when we see our reflection in someone else's face or see that person's reaction toward us, we use the information to determine our self-worth (Schiraldi, 1993). Thus, self-esteem might be more appropriately called "other-esteem." No one develops self-esteem apart from the inputs they receive from others— it results from your perception of the other individual's opinion of you.

- If self-esteem results from our perception of another's opinion of us, consider how this truth might impact the self-esteem of ministers entering retirement.

- If you feel required to retire (i.e., your decision was NOT voluntary), how would that affect your self-esteem?

- If you retire with little or no anticipation of future ministry, how might that affect your self-esteem?

- If you retire in a culture (e.g., the North American culture) that neglects valuing the wisdom that comes with age, how would that affect your self-esteem?

- If you find that all your past friends grow emotionally distant and less interested in you than previously anticipated, how would that affect your self-esteem?

- If you suddenly perceive that your peers, fellow ministers, agency's leaders, other chaplains, or your home church, no longer value your ministry or input, how would that affect your self-esteem?

Due to the above factors, retirement frequently affects the self-esteem of a minister (especially a missionary or chaplain) more than it affects secular individuals who transition into retirement. The minister's self-esteem is damaged largely due to the negative image held by others.

Fundamental Truth:
We lack self-esteem only because we believe a lot of
things that are untrue! (Schiraldi, 1993)

This negative self-image is fueled by chronic untrue beliefs that are sometimes reinforced by the retirement transition process itself.

Some common false beliefs among retirement age ministers include:

- Others should love and accept me. Ministers sometimes believe that others should welcome their skills into their sphere of influence and love them simply because they are retired ministers. However, without an extremely close personal relationship, this remains an unrealistic expectation. Without an already existing close relationship, no basis exists for others to love and accept us. If we—as Christians and ministers—sometimes, ourselves, find difficulty loving and accepting our fellow co-workers, how realistic can we expect those who know us less will love and accept us more?

- No one loves me. In contrast to the above belief, ministers entering retirement sometimes believe that no one loves them. This, too, is false. No one knows the total sphere of influence that you developed over a lifetime of ministry. Thus, it is unrealistic to assume that no one loves the retiring minister, missionary, or chaplain simply because he or she is unable to see that love first-hand. Many Christians prayed for the retiring minister over a period of decades. Such dedication is a Christ-like love. And, regardless of the love of others, God loves us enough that He called us into service with Him.

- Others should recognize and value me. Ministers sometimes believe that others should automatically value them and their potential future ministry. However, without an extremely close relationship, this probably remains an unrealistic expectation. Others possess little basis on which to value a missionary's potential contribution to an American church culture. Although peers may value and recognize a minister, it remains unrealistic to expect strangers to recognize and value him or her in the same way. They simply don't know his or her ministry that well. The missionary or chaplain may accumulate a wealth of wisdom in another culture, but few may recognized or valued it elsewhere.

- I should always please others (live up to their expectations of me). Some ministers believe that they should always succeed at pleasing others. During retirement transition, such a person endeavors to live up to the unspoken and unrealistic expectations of others. By trying to live up to the expectations of others, this person feels hampered in working through his or her personal transition issues. This attitude places others in full control of the minister facing retirement, and leads to an unrealistically low self-esteem.

- There is something wrong with me. Ministers pushed into retirement almost always conclude that something is wrong with them. Usually, their error results from believing that something is wrong with them, personally, instead of realizing that a failed relationship, or an illness, or some other contributing factor might have prompted their forced retirement. Regardless, almost all ministers eventually feel that something is wrong with them simply because they experience emotional numbness, loss of appetite, loss of sleep, guilt, loss of concentration, and loss of energy during the retirement transition. These feelings seem surprising. However, the belief that something is wrong with them remains a misperception. These are normal feelings for a very abnormal event. The event, not the feeling, is abnormal.

- I am defective and inferior to other people. Almost all ministers transitioning into retirement feel inferior to those still employed. The retiring minister, however, possesses many skills that have been honed over decades of ministry. The challenge is to find new ways to use those skills instead of lingering in an emotional state of inferiority. God values each individual equally, including the one who may feel handicapped by age or physical problems. God values all, equally. No inferior retiree exists in the Kingdom. The apostle Paul exclaimed, "I have kept the faith, I have finished the course." As a joint heir with Christ, you are an overcomer.

- I am hopeless—there is no future ministry for me. Retirement transition can easily leave you feeling defeated. The number and gravity of retirement decisions can seem overwhelming. However, they are never too big for God. He gives us countless friends and helpers with whom we can interact for support and additional insights. With Christ at our helm, hope flourishes. Even as we retire, a future ministry awaits. These three remain: faith, hope, and love.

- I should always be respected and viewed as perfect. Missionaries and other ministers are often put on a super-spiritual pedestal of near-sainthood by individuals in their local church. In fact, in some church cultures, a minister can easily start believing the expectations of the local church members. Subsequently, as they start to feel anger and resentment during the retirement transition process, they feel guilty of their angry emotions, stemming from the belief that they should be perfect. They fail to accept that they remain merely human, not yet perfectly sanctified. The truth is that while everyone wants absolute perfection, we continue a journey of spiritual growth. No minister attains perfection this side of heaven.

- I am unworthy and a wretched sinner. Many Christians, including ministers, at times may believe that they are unworthy, filthy, and wretched. The truth is that we all WERE unworthy, filthy, and wretched. However, we are now joint-heirs with Christ. We are no longer unworthy and filthy any more than our joint-heir, Jesus himself, is unworthy and filthy. We are now spotless, redeemed, and made worthy through the blood of the Lamb.

The Bible invalidates each of the common false beliefs in the preceding list. The following laws have been adapted and edited for style from Howard's Laws as described in Building Self-Esteem, A 125 Day Program (Schiraldi, 1993, 25). Using your Bible and concordance, please search for at least two Scripture verses that substantiate the following laws of unconditional worth before God:

- God values you infinitely and eternally.

Scripture #1:

Scripture # 2:

How has God shown you that He values you infinitely and eternally?

- God values each individual equally. Therefore, the following externals neither add to nor diminish our worth:

Our market worth (how much money we can earn)

Scripture #1:

Scripture # 2:

Our social worth (how many friends esteem us)

Scripture #1:

Scripture # 2:

Our ability to perform or accomplish tasks

Scripture #1:

Scripture # 2:

How has God shown you that He values each individual equally?

- Your worth is complete in Christ, but it is not completed.

Scripture #1:

Scripture # 2:

How has God shown you that your worth is complete in Christ, but not completed?

- God's assessment of your eternal value never changes (even if someone else rejects you, or when—not *if*—you fail).

  Scripture #1:

  Scripture #2:

- How has God shown you that His assessment of your eternal value never changes?

- God never stops pursuing you and your children.

  Scripture #1:

  Scripture # 2:

- How has God shown you that He never stops pursuing you or your children?

For example, I was taught that God never stops pursuing his children through the following personal experience:

As a nine-year-old missionary kid (MK), I remember itinerating in Arkansas with my parents. During itineration, my parents gave out hundreds of prayer cards. Each card included a small black-and-white photo of our family along with our names and the country to which we were going.

Like many MKs, I rejected Christianity in my early twenties and didn't come back to God until my early thirties. Finally, at 52 years of age, I became a missionary and was invited to participate in the

Pennsylvania mission's tour. When I arrived at a small country church, an elderly lady asked me, "Are you related to missionary Jim Davis from Arkansas?"

"Yes," I replied, "He is my father. Why do you ask?" From her purse, she pulled out a prayer card with our family photo. I was a nine-year-old child in the photo.

She noted that my father gave her the prayer card 43 years ago while he itinerated in Arkansas. Shortly afterward, her husband's employer transferred them to Pennsylvania, and she never knew what happened to our family. However, her most remarkable statement came at the end of her explanation, "So, I came today hoping let you know that I have been praying for you every day."

I choked back the tears as I reflected on God's pursuit of me throughout my life. I learned a lesson, first-hand, about His persistence— God never stops pursuing His children. And, His disciples never stop loving each other, either. That old saint from Pennsylvania prayed for me for over forty years, never knowing what had happened to me. She proved that many unknown Christians love me almost as much as my heavenly Father does. She was overjoyed to learn how God had answered her faithful prayers.

Reflection: If self-esteem comes from seeing a reflection of ourselves as we look at others, describe the kind of self-esteem that is possible when we look toward other Christians, including our mission leaders, other pastors, and other ministers?

Reflection: If self-esteem comes from seeing a reflection of ourselves as we look at others, describe the kind of self-esteem that is possible if we fail to look toward God, i.e., fail to have daily devotional time with Him?

Summary Reflection: Where is the only correct source from whom we can obtain accurate self-esteem? What specific plans will you make to ensure that you constantly look toward that source for your self-esteem?

Fundamental Truths

1. *We lack self-esteem only because we believe a lot of things that are untrue (Schiraldi, 1993)!*

2. *We cannot value the self if we do not spend time with the One (God) who values us in truth.*

   Reflection: On average, it takes approximately five validations to counteract a single invalidation. Thus, if we receive even a single invalidation during the retirement transition:

   - What is the probability that we will receive at least five validations from fellow Christians to counteract each and every instance of invalidation?
   - What is the probability that we will maintain a healthy self-image if we do not spend time with God in daily devotions?

3. *You are all sons of God through faith in Christ Jesus, for all of you who were baptized into Christ have clothed yourselves with Christ. There is neither Jew nor Greek, slave nor free, male nor female, for*

you are all one in Christ Jesus. If you belong to Christ, then you are Abraham's seed, and heirs according to the promise. (Galatians 3:26-29)

4. *So you are no longer a slave, but a son; and since you are a son, God has made you also an heir. (Galatians 4:7)*

Reflection: Self-esteem is based on an accurate and honest appraisal of our strengths and weaknesses. Consider the following actions:

- Acknowledge your weaknesses. My weaknesses are:

- Announce your weaknesses to others. They will notice your weaknesses, anyway, even if you fail to announce them! So, it is best simply to announce them—it enables others to determine how to best adjust to your weaknesses. How can you go about announcing your particular weaknesses?

- Acknowledge that everyone else in the world is also flawed and imperfect. Whom have you held in esteem, possibly above the level that they deserve?

- Love yourself, with your faults, even as Christ loves you. What are some faults that you pledge to acknowledge, even while still loving yourself?

- Accept and forgive yourself without condition, even as Christ accepts and forgives you with your faults. This is the key to positive change and growth. Faults and actions for which I need to forgive myself include:

- Acknowledge that personal change and growth result from spending time with God. Personal change and growth are not a matter of your willpower. All you can do is spend time with the One who causes personal and spiritual growth. In March, 2006, a Newsweek reporter asked Dr. Billy Graham, "If a young evangelist asked you how much time he should spend on politics versus purely pastoral work, what would you say?" Dr. Graham replied, "In my own life it's been a mixture. I've been concerned about our nation, our world and the political processes, but also I have regretted that I have not spent more time in prayer ...To a young man today, I would say: "Put your emphasis on your Bible study and prayer."

  At what time of each day will you commit to spend time with God?

How much time each day will you commit to spend with God?

What other spiritual disciplines will you adopt as a means of developing your relationship with God?

Successful retirement transition always results in personal and spiritual growth.

APPENDICES

Appendix A: Other Helps

Creative Retirement and Lifelong Learning Programs—see www.unca.edu/ncccr/Links/index.htm

Osher Lifelong Learning Institute, George Mason University

The Encore Center for Lifelong Enrichment, NC State University, Raleigh NC

Center for Creative Retirement, Sandhills Community College, Pinehurst NC

Center for Lifelong Learning, Blue Ridge Community College, Flat Rock NC

UNCG Emeritus Society, Division of Continual Learning, UNCG, Greensboro NC

Vital Aging Network, University of Minnesota, Twin Cities MN

The Harvard Institute for Learning in Retirement, Cambridge, MA

The Institute for Retired Professionals of the New School University, New York NY

Center for Lifelong Learning at University of Texas - El Paso TX

The Christopher Wren Association at the College of William and Mary, Williamsburg VA

Institute for Lifelong Education at Dartmouth, Hanover, NH

Learning in Retirement Institute at George Mason University, Fairfax, VA

Southern Delaware Academy of Lifelong Learning, University of
    Delaware

Creative Retirement Center, International College, Naples FL

North Carolina Center for Creative Retirement, Asheville NC

Center for Creative Retirement, College of Charleston, Charleston SC

Creative Retirement Institute, Edmonds Community College, Lynnwood
    WA

Creative   Retirement   Manitoba,   Winnipeg,   MB   Canada

Appendix B: Legal Documents

Since requirements for the following legal documents differ for each state of residence, please check with an attorney for your state requirements.

Personal Will:

1. A will is your opportunity to specify who gets what, when, and where. *If you don't have a will*, the state will have one for you (but without your input)!

2. Your will should be drawn now and updated as needed to include births, deaths, marriages, and changes in status.

Community Property Agreement:

1. A Community Property Agreement allows for the immediate transfer of all assets from one spouse to the other in the event of one's death. Some states use this document; others do not; and documents differ from state to state. Ask your attorney.

2. A Community Property Agreement is only valid between spouses, and cannot be considered as a replacement for a will.

A Living Will:

1. A Living Will provides instructions to family and physicians about what should be done—or not done—in the event you are unable to make or communicate a decision about your medical treatment. The main purpose of a Living Will is to make sure a person is not kept alive in a vegetative state on life-support systems.

2. Many states permit Living Wills. However, laws differ from state to state, even among those permitting such a will, so it is wise to make local inquiry.

Durable Power of Attorney for Health Care:

1. States that do not allow for a Living Will may make provision for a Durable Power of Attorney for Health Care. This would basically accomplish the same purpose as a Living Will. One of the values of preparing this sort of will is that you can express your desire to your family. Many individuals give the power of attorney to their spouse.

2. By expressing your desires in a written form, you can save your family the anxiety of making decisions for you when you cannot make them yourself.

DURABLE POWER OF ATTORNEY

BEFORE EXECUTING THIS DOCUMENT YOU SHOULD KNOW THESE IMPORTANT FACTS:

Except as you specify otherwise in this document, this document gives the person you designate as your agent (the attorney-in-fact) the power to make a broad range of financial and property decisions for you during your life when you are no longer capable of making such decisions for yourself. Your agent must act consistently with your desires as stated in this document or otherwise made known. The signing of this document should be witnessed by two disinterested parties and notarized by a notary public.

By initialing the proper box in Section 2 of this form, you must choose the event upon which this durable power of attorney takes effect. First, you may choose to allow the power of attorney to be effective immediately. In such cases, the power of attorney will continue until formally terminated by you and will stay in effect through the course of any periods of incompetence or disability. Unless found incompetent or disabled by your regular attending physician, you will still have the right to make financial and property decisions for yourself, but your attorney-in-fact will also have such powers. The other option is to have the power of attorney become effective only upon written evidence of incompetence or disability by your regular attending physician. In such cases, you alone will have the right to make financial and property decisions for yourself until you are formally determined to be incompetent or disabled. At that time, your attorney-in-fact will receive the power to make such decisions on your behalf.

This document gives your agent complete financial and disposition authority over the following matters as if you were making the decisions yourself: safe deposit boxes, real property, personal property, financial accounts, United States treasury bonds, moneys due, claims against you, legal proceedings, written instruments, and tax returns. If you do not want your agent to have authority over one or more of these areas, you must mark through that specific portion of the document in Section 3 of the form, initial, and date that mark prior to your signature on that document.

Initialing the proper boxes in Section 4 of the form may activate optional powers of your attorney-in-fact. These optional powers include the ability to make charitable gifts on your behalf, to establish and transfer assets to trusts on your behalf, to disclaim any property in which you otherwise hold rights, to transfer assets in order to qualify you for medical assistance or benefits programs, and to direct the disposition of property at your death.

The attorney-in-fact is entitled to reimbursement for reasonable expenses incurred in the performance of duties on your behalf. An accounting of all actions taken by the attorney-in-fact for or on behalf of you and your estate may be required at any time by you, a guardian of your estate, or the executor of your estate.

This power of attorney may be terminated in three ways: (1) written notice of termination from you to the attorney-in-fact, (2) termination by the guardian of your estate after court approval of the termination, or (3) your death (when the attorney-in-fact receives actual knowledge or written notice of your death).

Your agent may need this document immediately in case of an emergency that requires decisions concerning your finances or property. Either keep this document or copies of this document where it is immediately available to your agent and alternate agents or give each of them an executed copy of this document. You may also want to give your financial advisors a copy of this document.

Durable Power of Attorney

01. Designation. I, _____(the
"Principal") designate

____ _____as   attorney-in-
fact for the Principal.

If the designated attorney-in-fact fails to qualify, ceases to act or is
unwilling to serve, then _____   is
designated as attorney-in-fact for Principal.

02. Effectiveness: Duration. *[Principal must initial in the
affirmative (yes) either 2.1 or 2.2. The one not initialed in the
affirmative (yes) should be initialed in the negative (no).]* This
power of attorney:

_____ _____ **2.1** Shall become effective immediately, shall
Yes   No   not be affected by the disability or
                 incompetence of the Principal, and shall
                 continue until revoked or terminated under
                 Section 5, notwithstanding any uncertainty
                 as to whether the Principal is dead or alive.

_____ _____ **2.2** Shall not become effective until written
Yes   No   evidence of incompetence or of the
                 determination of disability is made by the
                 Principal's regular attending physician.
                 This power of attorney shall continue until
                 revoked or terminated under section 5,

notwithstanding any uncertainty as to whether the Principal is dead or alive. Disability shall include the inability to manage property and affairs effectively for reasons such as mental illness, mental deficiency, physical illness or disability, advanced age, chronic use of drugs, chronic intoxication, confinement, detention by a foreign power or disappearance.

3. **Powers.** The attorney-in-fact shall have all of the powers of an absolute owner over the assets and liabilities of the Principal, wherever located. These powers shall include, without limitation, the power and authority specified below.

    3.1 Safe Deposit Box. The attorney-in-fact shall have access at all times to remove the content of any safe deposit box which the Principal has a right of access.

    3.2 Real Property. The attorney-in-fact shall have authority to purchase, take possession of, lease, sell, convey, exchange, mortgage, release and encumber real property or any interest in real property.

    3.3 Personal Property. The attorney-in-fact shall have authority to purchase, receive, take possession of, lease, sell, assign, endorse, exchange, release, mortgage and pledge personal property or any interest in personal property.

    3.4 Financial Accounts. The attorney-in-fact shall have the authority to deal with accounts maintained by or on behalf of the Principal with institutions (including, without limitation, banks, savings and loan associations, credit unions and securities dealers). This shall include the authority to maintain and close existing accounts, to open, maintain and close other accounts, and to make deposits, transfers, and withdrawals with respect to all such accounts.

3.5 United States Treasury Bonds. The attorney-in-fact shall have the authority to purchase United States Treasury Bonds which may be redeemed at par in payment of federal estate tax.

3.6 Moneys Due. The attorney-in-fact shall have the authority to request, demand, recover, collect, endorse and receive all moneys, debts, accounts, gifts, bequests, dividends, annuities, rents and payments due the Principal.

3.7 Claims Against Principal. The attorney-in-fact shall have authority to pay, settle, compromise or otherwise discharge any and all claims of liability or indebtedness against the Principal and, in so doing, use any of the Principal's funds or other assets or use funds or other assets of the attorney-in-fact and obtain reimbursement out of the Principal's funds or other assets.

3.8 Legal Proceedings. The attorney-in-fact shall have authority to participate in any legal action in the name of the Principal or otherwise. This shall include (a) actions for attachment, execution, eviction, foreclosure, indemnity, and any other proceeding for equitable or injunctive relief and (b) legal proceedings in connection with the authority granted in the instrument.

3.9 <u>Written Instruments</u>. The attorney-in-fact shall have the power and authority to sign, seal, execute, deliver and estate acknowledge all written instruments and do and perform each and every act and thing whatsoever which may be necessary or proper in the exercise of the powers and authority granted to the attorney-in-fact as fully as the Principal could do if personally present.

3.10 <u>Tax Returns</u>. The attorney-in-fact may prepare and sign on Principal's behalf and in name any and all tax returns, federal, state or local which Principal may be required to file.

04. Optional Powers. By initialing the following optional provisions, in the affirmative (yes), the Principal authorizes the attorney-in-fact to:

_____ _____ **4.1** Make charitable gifts based on Principal's
Yes   No   expressed desires stated while competent, the pattern of giving by the Principal during management of their own affairs and/or the percentage such charitable gifts, made by the Principal during their management, relative to the Principal's income and assets.

_____ _____ **4.2** Transfer assets of all kinds to the trustee of
Yes   No   any trust which trust was established by Principal and, if not established by Principal, a trust which is for the sole benefit of the Principal, and which

terminates at the Principal's death with the Principal's property distributable to the executor of the Principal's estate.

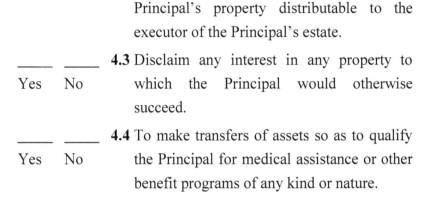

_____ _____ **4.3** Disclaim any interest in any property to
Yes   No   which the Principal would otherwise succeed.

_____ _____ **4.4** To make transfers of assets so as to qualify
Yes   No   the Principal for medical assistance or other benefit programs of any kind or nature.

0**5.** **Termination.** This power of attorney may be terminated by:

(a) The Principal by written notice to the attorney-in-fact and, if this power of attorney has been recorded, by recording the written instrument of revocation in the office of the recorder or auditor of the place where the power was recorded;

(b) A Guardian of the estate of the Principal after court approval of such revocation; or

(c) The death of the Principal upon actual knowledge or receipt of written notice by the attorney-in-fact.

0**6.** **Accounting.** Upon request of the Principal or the Guardian of the estate of the Principal or the executor of the Principal's estate, the attorney-in-fact shall account for all actions taken by the attorney-in-fact for or on behalf of the Principal.

0**7.** **Expenses/Compensation.** My attorney-in-fact herein appointed, or any successor, shall be entitled to reimbursement for his or her reasonable expenses incurred in the performance of his or her duties.

08. Reliance. Any person acting without negligence and in good faith in reasonable reliance on this power of attorney shall not incur any liability thereby. Any action taken, unless otherwise invalid or unenforceable, shall be binding on the heirs and representatives of the Principal.

09. Indemnity. The estate of the Principal shall hold harmless and indemnify the attorney-in-fact from all liability for acts done in good faith and not in fraud of the Principal.

10. Severance and Validity. In the event any power or authority given herein by the Principal to the attorney-in-fact cannot be exercised under the laws of the State where executed, or under the laws of another State where this Durable Power of Attorney is being utilized, the remaining powers and authorities hereunder granted shall remain in full force and effect and shall in no way be affected, impaired or invalidated thereby.

11. Applicable Law. The laws of the State where executed shall govern this power of attorney.

12. Disability of Principal. This Power of Attorney shall not be affected by the Principal's subsequent disability or incapacity and shall remain effective for an unlimited period after the disability or incapacity occurs.

13. Photocopies. Any person relying on this Power of Attorney may rely on a photocopy as if it were an original.

Principal

Witness

Witness

STATE OF _____)
) ss.
COUNTY OF _____)

On this the _____ day of _____, 20___, before me, the undersigned Notary Public, personally appeared _____ known to me to be the person described in and who executed the foregoing instrument, and acknowledged to me that he or she signed and sealed said instrument as his or her free and voluntary act and deed for the uses and purposes therein mentioned.

IN WITNESS WHEREOF I have hereunto set my hand and affixed my official seal the day and year first above written.

_____

Notary Public in and for the state of _____
residing at _____
My commission expires: _____

THIS IS A LEGAL DOCUMENT. YOU SHOULD READ IT CAREFULLY AND SEEK LEGAL COUNSEL

Appendix C: Data for Family File

Please collect the following documents and family data, now. Then note alongside your list where the documents are kept.

Estate Planning

Wills
Trust agreements
Powers of attorney
Retirement
investment agreements

Family

Birth certificates
Marriage licenses
Divorce papers
Adoption papers
Social Security numbers
Military discharge papers
VA claim number
Employee ID number
Naturalization papers

Personal Property

Inventory of all bank accounts
Certificates of deposit
Vehicle registration
Broker accounts
Investment accounts
Designations of desire for disposal of personal items

Real Property

Deeds
Buy/sell agreements
Mortgage agreements

Taxes/Tax Returns

U.S. and state returns (including audits) for last three years
Current year information
Gifts/designations

Business

Canceled checks for last three years
Contracts, agreements for assets owned
Employee pension/profit-sharing
Safe deposit box: location, number, and both keys

Insurance

Home
Life
Health/accident
Disability
Annuities

Notes/Obligations

Inventory of those payable/ receivable

Appendix D: Internal Revenue Service (IRS)

1. Keep accurate and detailed records. This is absolutely essential!

2. Be sure to take all the deductions that are allowed to ministers.

3. If you work with and receive reimbursement from a church or a church-related organization, making a reimbursement agreement with them is helpful for tax time. (See suggested forms on the following pages.)

4. If you are employed by a church or a church-related organization and are receiving _only_ _a housing allowance_ from them or a housing allowance plus an "accountable" reimbursement of auto and professional expenses, the church should not fill out a W-2 or W-4 form in your name for these amounts, since they are not _income_-taxable. Any additional salary should be reported on a W-2 or 1099MISC, depending on the employment relationship between you and the church.

5. Your Social Security checks may be taxable to you. If all your taxable income (including the foreign earned income exclusion) plus up to 50% of your Social Security payments are in excess of $25,000 (single) or ($32,000) couple, you will have to pay income tax on a portion of your Social Security payments.

6. The maximum amount of earned income on which Social Security/self-employment tax is computed is $97,500 for 2007. Above that amount, the Medicare percentage is 2.9%. There is no limit on the earnings on which you pay Medicare tax.

7. Sources of helpful information:

Church and Clergy Tax Guide by Richard Hammar, J.D., LL.M., CPA. Available through Gospel Publishing House, Springfield, Missouri, and Christian bookstores, approximate cost: $20.00.

A very comprehensive guide to tax issues and church-related reporting, tapes, and newsletters is available at www.churchlawtoday.com.

Church Law & Tax Report, Christianity Today International, 465 Gunderson Dr., Sarol Tream IL, 60188, 800-222-1840.

The Zondervan Minister's Tax & Financial Guide by Daniel D. Busby, CPA. Approximate Cost: $16.00.

8. A tax return transcript can be ordered from the IRS at 1-800-829-1040. This will give you the tax information as reported on the tax return. If you desire a copy of the return, the IRS charges $39.00 and you must file a form 4506 and mail it to the service center where the return was originally filed. Allow 30-60 days for delivery.

Housing Allowance and Remuneration Agreements:

If you become employed by a church or church-related organization, it will be to your advantage to make a financial agreement with that organization concerning housing allowance and reimbursement of car and professional expenses. Such an agreement will enable you to obtain all the IRS benefits to which you are entitled as a minister of the gospel.

Following are copies of two forms that may be used by a local church:

Minister's Estimate of Housing Expense

To: (name of church)

From: (name of minister)

Subject: Housing Allowance for (year)

The amounts set forth below are an estimate of the expenses I expect to incur during _____(date)_____ in providing a home.

ITEM
                AMOUNT

1.   Rent on living premises, or $

2.   Principal and interest on home mortgage loan

3.   Real estate taxes

4.   Utilities (gas, electricity, oil, coal, wood,
          water, sewer, garbage, telephone, but not long
          distance—etc.)

5.   Insurance

6.   Repairs and maintenance

7.   Furniture and furnishings

8.   Other housing expenses

Date_____   _____
                                                    Signature

**The housing allowance adjustment to income cannot exceed the lesser of (1) the fair rental value of your home, furnished, plus utilities, (2) the actual amount spent on housing, or (3) the estimated housing allowance amount.

SAMPLE COPY

COMPENSATION RESOLUTION

Date: _____ 20____

Total Compensation

A motion was made by _____ and seconded by _____ and carried that the total compensation to be expended for Reverend _____ for the calendar year 20____ is $_____.

<u>Housing</u>

The Chairman informed the meeting that under the law, a minister of the gospel is not subject to federal income tax on "housing allowance paid to him or her as part of his or her compensation to the extent used by him or her to rent or provide a home." After considering the estimate of Reverend _____ of his home expenses, a motion was made by _____ and seconded by _____ and carried that of the total compensation for the year <u>20</u>___, $_____ is hereby designated as "housing allowance." This designation shall remain in effect until canceled or changed.

<u>Automobile Reimbursement</u>

A motion was made by _____ and seconded by _____ and carried that a further amount of total compensation be reimbursement for auto expenses for Reverend _____ to the extent used by him or her for pastoral and other ministerial duties and supported by documentation and submitted to the church. Estimated reimbursement for his auto expenses shall be $_____.

Professional Expenses Reimbursement

A motion was made by _____ and seconded by _____ and carried that all professional expenses be reimbursed to Reverend _____ from total compensation. Estimated professional expenses for 20_____ shall be $_____.

Signed

_____

(Recording Secretary)

Signed

_____

(Pastor)

Auto Expenses: Suggested Format

An auto expense book is a necessary IRS tool if you are employed by a church or a church-related institution.

For the expenses of ministry to be deductible, the IRS requires that you keep a day-to-day record of church-related car expenses. (Only those expenses related to the ministry are deductible. Commuting to and from the church or office are never deductible.)

The IRS allows a cents-per-mile or actual vehicle expenses related to ministry. Licensing, car repairs, and insurance are also tax-deductible to the extent you use the vehicle for business. These expenses must be prorated for business use.

Other Expenses:

The following form could be used for reporting monthly expenses while serving on staff at a church.

At the end of each month, make copies of all receipts and complete this form in duplicate. One form, together with copies of the receipts, is submitted to the church treasurer so that you can be reimbursed for expenses. The original receipts are stapled to the other form and retained in the minister's personal file.

Managing Retirement Funds:

1. Inventory your present worth and your retirement needs.

2. If you will need to supplement your income, examine your skills and don't be afraid to use them.

3. Take a look at what other retired ministers are doing to supplement income:

a. Larger churches hire retired ministers for staff positions, particularly for senior adult ministries and visitation ministries.

b. Christian schools need foreign language teachers.

c. Good 35mm pictures are sometimes marketable, as are artifacts.

d. Do you like to travel? Act as a tour guide to your part of the world, and use this as a means of promoting missions.

Three Things to Remember:

1. *Both* husband and wife should be knowledgeable about everything that has to do with family finances, insurance, etc.

2. *Both* husband and wife should have credit cards, and the wife's card should be in her *own* name (Mary Smith, <u>not</u> Mrs. John Smith). Both cards can have the same number and the billings can come to the one account. *Separate names are necessary to establish a credit rating for the wife in case of the husband's death.*

3. Some ministers have been tempted to draw their agency-held retirement funds in one lump sum and put them into mutual funds or elsewhere to receive a higher interest rate. *Remember,* however, that in so doing, while you may be able to roll the funds into a higher interest bearing account, you will lose the advantage of drawing these funds by the month designated as "housing," thus remaining tax-sheltered. Also, investing your entire retirement fund in equities may be risky when there is a market downturn. If

the spouse is not a credentialed minister, he or she will not receive the retirement funds as minister's housing.

Appendix E: References

Adler, M. (2001). "Conceptualizing and Measuring Appreciation: The development of a new positive psychology construct." *Dissertation Abstracts International*, 63, 08B.

Augsburger, David. *Dissident Discipleship: A Spirituality Of Self-Surrender, Love Of God, And Love Of Neighbor*. Grand Rapids, MI: Brazos Press, 2006

Blumenthal, J. A., Babyak, M. A., Moore, K. A., Craighead, W. E., Herman, S., Khatri, P, et al. (1999). "Effects of exercise training on older patients with major depression." *Archives of Internal Medicine*, 159, 2349-2356.

Bridges, William. *Transitions: Making Sense of Life's Changes*. Reading, MA: Perseus Books Publishing: 1980.

Burns, David D. *The Feeling Good Book*. New York: Plume: 1999.

Buss, D. M. (2000). "The Evolution of Happiness." *American Psychologist*, 55 (1), 15-22.

Cohen, Gene D., *The Creative Age: Awakening Human Potential in the Second Half of Life*. NY: Harper-Collins, 2000.

Cohen, L. H., McGowan, J., Fooskas, S., & Rose, S. (1984). "Positive life events and social support and the relationship between life stress and psychological disorder." *American Journal of Community Psychology*, 12, 567-587.

Cordian, L., Gotshall, R. W., Eaton, S. B. & Eaton. S. B. (1998). 'Physical Activity, Energy Expenditure And Fitness: An Evolutionary Perspective," *International Journal of Sports Medicine*, 19, 328-335.

De Mello M. F., de Jesus Mari J., Bacaltchuk J., Verdeli H., & Neugebauer R. (2005). "A Systematic Review Of Research Findings On The Efficacy On Interpersonal Therapy For Depressive Disorders." *European Archives of Psychiatry and Clinical Neuroscience*, 255, 75-82.

Dimidjian, S., Hollon, S. D., Dobson, K. S., Schmaling, K. B., Kohlenberg, R. J., Addis, M. E., et al. (2006). "Randomized Trial Of

Behavioral Activation, Cognitive Therapy, And Antidepressant Medication In The Acute Treatment Of Adults With Major Depression." *Journal of Consulting and Clinical Psychology*, 74 (4), 658-670.

Elkin, I., Shea, T., Watkins, J. T., Imber, S. D., Sotsky, S. M., Collins, J. F., et al (1989). "National Institute of Mental Health Treatment of Depression Collaborative Research Program." *Archives of General Psychiatry*, 46, 971-982.

Emmons, Robert A., *The Psychology of Ultimate Concerns: Motivation and Spirituality in Personality.* NY: The Guilford Press, 1999.

Freudenheim, Ellen. *Looking Forward, An Optimist's Guide to Retirement.* Stewart, NY, NY: Tabori, and Chang, 2004.

Johnson, Sharon L. *Therapist's Guide to Clinical Intervention: The 123s of Treatment Planning.* San Diego, CA: Academic Press, 1997.

Johnson, Spencer. *The Present : The Secret to Enjoying Your Work And Life, Now!* USA, DoubleDay, 2003

Just, N., & Alloy, L. B. (1997). "The Response Styles Theory Of Depression: Tests And An Extension Of The Theory.' *Journal of Abnormal Psychology*, 106, 221-229.

Harris, I and associates. *The Myth and Reality of Aging in America.* Washington DC: The National Council on Aging, Inc., 1975.

Hibbleln, J. R., and Salem, N. (1995). "Dietary Polyunsaturated Fatty Acids And Depression: When Cholesterol Does Not Satisfy." *American Journal of Clinical Nutrition*, 62, 1-9.

Hill, R. D., Storandt, M., & Mappey, M. (1993). "The Impact Of Long-Term Exercise Training On Psychological Function In Older Adults." *Journal of Gerontology*: Psychological Sciences, 48, 12-17.

Ilardi, S., Karwoski, L., Lehman, K., Stites, B., & Steidtmann, D. (2007). "We Were Never Designed For This: The Depression Epidemic And The Promise Of Therapeutic Lifestyle Change," preprint copy, Lawrence KS: University of Kansas.

Kirpke, D. F. (1998). "Light Treatment For Nonseasonal Depression: Speed, Efficacy And Combined Treatment." *Journal of Affective Disorders*, 49, 109-117.

Kuller, R. (2002). "The Influence Of Light On Circahythms On Humans." *Journal of physiological anthropology and applied human science*, 21, 87-91.

Lazarus, Richard. (2006). "Prelude to a Theme on Emotion and Gratitude." *Journal of Personality*, 74:1.

Macionis, J. J. *Sociology: Annotated Instructor's Edition* (7th Ed.). Upper Saddle River, NJ: Prentice Hall, 1999.

Morawetz, D. (2003). "Insomnia And Depression: Which Comes First?" *Sleep Research Online*, 5, 77-81.

National Institute of Mental Health (NIMH). (1999). The Numbers Count (NIH Publication No NIH 99-4584).

Nemets, B., Stahl, Z., & Belmaker, R. H. (2002). "Addition Of Omega-3 Fatty Acid To Maintenance Medication Treatment For Recurrent Unipolar Depressive Disorder." *American Journal of Psychiatry*, 159, 477-479.

Nemets, H., Nemets, B., Apter, A., Bracha, Z., & Belmaker, R. H. (2006). "Omega-3 Treatment Of Childhood Depression; A Controlled Double-Blind Pilot Study." *American Journal of Psychiatry*, 163, 1098-1100.

Nolen-Hoeksema, S. (1991). "Responses To Depression And Their Effects On The Duration Of Depressive Episodes," *Journal of Abnormal Psychology*, 100 (4), 569-582.

Otterbour, Robert K. *Retire and Thrive: Remarkable People, Age 50-Plus, Share Their Creative, Productive & Profitable Retirement Strategies*. Washington DC: Kiplinger Books, 2003.

Peet, M., & Horrobin, D. F. (2002). "A Dose-Ranging Study Of The Effects Of Ethyleicosapentainoate In Patients With Ongoing Depression Despite Treatment With Apparently Adequate Treatment With Standard Drugs," *Archives of General Psychiatry*, 59, 913-919.

Peterson, E., *Working The Angles: The Shape Of Pastoral Integrity*. Grand Rapids MI: Eerdmans Publishing Co, 1987.

Pollock, David C. *The Transition Model, Seminar with David C. Pollock.* Bolder CO: Interaction Inc., 1988.

Ross, C. E., & Hayes, D. (1988). "Exercise And Psychologic Well-Being In The Community." *American Journal of Epidemiology*, 127, 762-771.

Rowe, John W., and Kahn, Robert L. *Successful Aging.* NY, NY: Dell, 1999.

Savishinsky, Joel S. *Breaking the Watch: The Meaning of Retirement in America.* Ithaca NY: Cornell University Press, 2000.

Schachter-Shalomi, Zalman. *From Age-ing to Sage-ing: A Profound New Vision of Growing Older.* NY, NY: Warner Books, 1997.

Schiraldi, Glenn R. *Building Self-Esteem: A 125 Day Program.* Ellicott City MD: Chevron Publishing Corp., 1993.

Snyder, C. R. (Ed.). *Book of Hope: Theory, Measures, and Applications.* USA: Academic Press, 2000.

Snyder, C. R. (Ed.), Lopez, Shane J. (Editor). *Book of Positive Psychology.* USA: Oxford University Press, 2002.

Snyder, C. R.. *The Psychology of Hope: You can get there from here.* New York: Free Press, 1994.

Stegner, Wallace. *Crossing to Safety.* NY, NY: Random House, Inc, 1986.

Stephens, T. (1988). "Physical Activity And Mental Health In The United States And Canada: Evidence From Four Population Surveys." *Preventative Medicine*, 17, 35-47.

Stokes, G. *On Being Old: The Psychology of Later Life.*, London: The Falmer Press, 1992.

Tunainen, A., Kripke, D. F., & Endo, T. (2004). "Light Therapy For Non-Seasonal Depression." *Cochrane Database System Review*, 2, CD004050.

Veroff, J., & Veroff, J.B. *Social Incentives: A Life-Span Developmental Approach*. New York, NY: Academic Press, 1980.

Wells, A., & Papageorgious, C. (2003). "Metacognitive Therapy For Rumination." In C. Papageorgiou (Ed.), *Depressive Rumination: Nature, Theory, And Treatment* (pp. 259-273). West Sussex, England: Wiley.

Yancey, Phillip. *What's So Amazing About Grace?* Zondervan: 2002.

Zelinski, Ernie J. *How to Retire Happy, Wild, and Free*. Berkeley, Calif: 10 Speed Press, 2005.

ABOUT THE AUTHORS

Nathan Davis
Beth Davis

In her primary role as Director of HealthCare Ministries, Beth leads teams that provide healthcare and medical resources world-wide. She is a board certified health care chaplain with a Doctor of Ministry degree. Prior to her marriage to Nathan, Beth served for 25 years as a missionary in Vietnam, the Philippines, Hong Kong, and Belgium.

Nathan grew up in Japan, the son of missionaries Dr. Jim and Genevieve Davis. Before becoming a missionary, Nathan served the US Air Force as a psychologist for 29 years. Nathan's primary role is facilitating seminars on relationship enhancement skills, crisis debriefing skills, spiritual formation, burnout prevention skills, stress management, and retirement transition issues. In the process of teaching preventative skills, Nathan and Beth consult each year those who seek confidential pastoral counseling on issues such as depression, anxiety, transition issues, marital stress, and conflict resolution.

Made in the USA
San Bernardino, CA
24 November 2015